ALSO BY ED SLOTT

Stay Rich for Life! Workbook
Your Complete Retirement Planning Road Map
The Retirement Savings Time Bomb . . . and How to Defuse It
Parlay Your IRA into a Family Fortune

STAY RICH

FOR

LIFE!

Growing & Protecting
Your Money in
Turbulent Times

ED SLOTT

BALLANTINE BOOKS NEW YORK

Published in the United States by Ballantine Books,
an imprint of The Random House Publishing Group,
a division of Random House, Inc., New York.

BALLANTINE and colophon are registered trademarks of Random House, Inc.

ISBN 978-0-345-51442-4

Printed in the United States of America on acid-free paper

www.ballantinebooks.com

8 9

Book design by Mary A. Wirth

To my wife, Linda and my children
Ilana, Rachel, and Jennifer

And to my mom

A Cautionary Note to Readers of
Stay Rich for Life!:

"Stay Rich for Life" is a commonsense approach to personal finance. In practical advice books, as in life, there are no guarantees, and readers are cautioned to rely on their own judgment about their individual circumstances and to act accordingly. Readers are also reminded that the approach described here is intended for informational purposes only and is not meant to take the place of professional advice. The laws in this area are complex and constantly changing. You should consult with an experienced professional to apply the relevant laws in your state to your unique situation.

In addition, I do not endorse, sell, or advise on investments or any financial products such as life insurance, annuities, mutual funds, stocks, bonds, or similar products and I have limited knowledge of these financial products. I am also not a partner or an owner of any company that sells or advises on investment products like the ones mentioned in the above sentence.

—ED SLOTT

A Cautionary Note Regarding Members of Ed Slott's Elite IRA Advisor Group™ and Ed Slott's Master Elite Advisor Group:

I have educated and trained these advisors on tax and estate planning, but I do not train them on financial products or investments. I am a tax advisor and not an investment advisor. I do not endorse any of the financial products or investments they sell or advise on. I do not sell these products and have limited financial product knowledge. I do not partner with any of these advisors, nor do I earn any income from sales of their products or services. They do pay our company an annual fee for the advanced education and training they receive year-round.

I am not responsible for investments or financial products or services you may purchase from any of these advisors. You should check all of their credentials.

—ED SLOTT

Contents

FIVE STEPS TO STAYING
RICH FOR LIFE

A message from Ed . . .

If you're like me, you may find yourself tempted to skip over a book's introductory material in the belief it's just fluff and dive straight to the chapters where the real "meat" is. But if you give in to that temptation, you will miss out on key information about how to use this book to secure your financial future. So, please read on. You have been advised!

What'd You *Do*?

I'll call her Sylvia. Some years back, when I was more active as a tax preparer, she came to me as April 15 approached for some help going over her tax returns. She told me that the previous fall she had been to a seminar on estate planning, where she'd learned about creating a living trust to protect her assets from going through probate—the court-supervised process of proving a will, appointing an executor, and settling an estate. Sylvia was eighty-five at the time and, not knowing how many years she had left, she thought the living trust was a very good idea. So she decided to do it.

Of course, a trust is worth nothing until you put something into it. Sylvia's largest asset was a tax-deferred $850,000 individual retirement account (IRA), and that's what she funded the trust with—putting the entire amount in. What she had not learned at the seminar (because it wasn't covered) and, therefore, was totally unaware of was this: With that simple transfer, she had unwittingly made the entire tax-deferred $850,000 accumulation suddenly vulnerable to taxation. I realized this when I spotted a Form 1099-R for a taxable $850,000 distribution in the papers she'd brought with her.

"What'd you *do*?" I asked. "You emptied your IRA!"

"No, I didn't," she replied. "I transferred it to a living trust."

"You can't do that," I said. "It's considered a withdrawal. Now you owe taxes on the whole kit and caboodle. You've got nothing to protect, except whatever will be left after Uncle Sam gets through with you."

As you might expect, Sylvia was beside herself at this news. In fact, I thought that day might turn out to be the final day of her eighty-five years, right there in my office. So I quickly added, "Maybe I can fix this"—even though I wasn't sure I could. This brought her back to life.

"The IRS will allow you to put the money back in your IRA within sixty days of taking it out and not be liable for withdrawal tax," I said. "When did you take it out?"

"Five months ago," she replied downheartedly.

"Okay, it's still a taxable distribution then," I said. "Unless . . ." I put my thinking cap on. Effective a year earlier, in 2002, the IRS had been granted the authority to waive the sixty-day rule in cases just like this one in which somebody with all good intentions had simply made a terrible error. The only way to take advantage of the waiver was to file what is called a Private Letter Ruling request for relief with the National Office of the Internal Revenue Service in Washington. It is a costly process—though not as costly as losing the bulk of her IRA to taxes would be if we made no request—and a time-consuming one. It took about nine months, but we got a favorable ruling and Sylvia was allowed to put all the money back into her IRA—no tax, no penalty; all was forgiven. She was able to undo her mistake. The IRS is not as liberal in these rulings as it once was, so today mistakes like this might not be fixed and that could result in losing a lifetime of savings for making one wrong move.

Over the years, and while touring the country with my Public Broadcasting Service special, I've heard many stories like Sylvia's, most of them with not-so-happy endings. It takes a long time to build up that kind of money, but it can be gone in a flash if, as the result of ignorance or poor advice, you're not extremely careful about when—and how—you move that money and use it. I refer to this problem as the "What'd you *do*?" syndrome because that's often how I react, as I did with Sylvia, when people relate their tales of woe about money and taxes to me.

I realized there was a huge void that needed to be filled to prevent investors and savers from doing dumb things as they try to build and preserve wealth—mistakes that can cost them big-time in taxes and trouble—and instead guide them to do smart things that can lead to staying rich for life.

So, I asked myself what it is that I do when I sit down with my clients and work with them to create a plan to protect their life savings for themselves and their families. And it suddenly hit me that I take them through five very specific steps—a blueprint, if you will—to real retirement savings success that works every time.

Furthermore, I was struck that while the focus of my own career has been on wealth preservation, these five steps are equally suited to creating a plan for *building* wealth. This is because the two disciplines, although separate, are part of the same overall equation.

Certainly managing taxes on investments is essential to staying rich for life, but you still need to get rich by first *building* your wealth the right way. So this book includes that information as well.

As I am primarily a tax advisor and expert on the retirement end of things, I took advantage of my extensive Rolodex of seasoned financial and legal professionals whom I have come to know in my travels and asked for their insights and advice on the broad areas of investment planning and wealth accumulation, estate planning, and insurance planning, not to mention special experience in the planning concerns of women and other niche areas. These are some of the most savvy, successful, and respected advisors in the nation, with hundreds of years of experience in their respective areas among them—literally the "best of the best."

You will benefit greatly from the candor and wisdom they offer throughout this book. And the reason I was able to get them to talk so openly is not just that they are colleagues and friends, but also that I agreed to quote most of them anonymously.

There's an old adage that from anonymity comes the truth. That may be right. But the main reason I agreed to anonymity for contributors to this book is compliance issues at their respective companies or in the financial services industry at large. Such regulations often restrict what advisors can say on the record in print, which typically leads to watered-down generalizations and sometimes muzzles them outright. But I have persuaded these professionals to spill the beans like never before so that you can benefit from their unfiltered knowledge and advice. And because I want you to know that they really exist, I have acknowledged all of them together, by name, in the Acknowledgments at the back of the book. Take a look—it's an impressive list!

Are You Ready for Some Football?

Think of financial security as a football game. The first half is the accumulation half. You work for, say, thirty or forty years, earning income. Some of that income you put aside for savings and investment. Assuming average investment results over the years, you're proud of what you've accomplished. You enjoy looking over the numbers when the statements come in, unless the market has tanked that month.

However, amassing a retirement fund is only half the game. At some point—probably when you are in your fifties or sixties—you'll stop working and the paychecks will likewise stop coming in. Then you may well have another thirty or forty years (or even longer) to live off that retirement fund you've built up. That's the second half of the game: the distribution half. If you don't play well in the third and fourth quarters, you'll wind up losing.

Some people play well in the first half, building up substantial amounts in their retirement accounts. However, they have no plan for the second half—the half during which money is withdrawn. In fact, most people don't even come out onto the field in the second half.

The IRS plays all four quarters, though. That's the government's plan. If you don't have your own plan, you'll be forced into the government's plan, the one whereby most of your retirement savings goes to the government, in the form of taxes.

What's more, scoring in the first half is much easier than winning the endgame. There are many resources out there to help you succeed in the first half. Your employer probably offers a retirement plan in which you can participate, setting aside today's income for tomorrow. There are many books, articles, TV shows, and websites telling you how to invest your money. Many financial advisors have enough knowledge and experience to guide you through a successful plan for building wealth. That's not the case for the second half of the game. What could go wrong? You might discover that the money you're withdrawing from your IRA won't go as far as you expected, after you pay tax. Thus, you might take out more money, to meet your living expenses. Before you know it, your IRA could be gone, long before you are. You could wind up watching your money carefully as you grow older, but better planning would have provided for the ability to meet your goals along the way, a comfortable retirement for yourself, and a sizable inheritance for your beneficiaries. You might have built enough to live well from now through retirement, but the money was lost to tax mistakes, made by you or by a financial advisor who was not educated about how to withdraw and use the money without triggering unnecessary taxes or penalties. Tax mistakes are tougher to stomach than market losses, since tax mistakes are within your control and can be avoided with proper planning and competent advice.

An alternate scenario: You could scrimp on spending now and throughout your retirement, denying yourself pleasurable experiences with your loved ones. This penny-pinching might enable you to leave a sizable estate—only to have most of it taxed away before your beneficiaries can enjoy this inheritance.

But getting the best of both worlds—building enough wealth to live comfortably now and through retirement as well as being able to leave a substantial legacy for your family—*can be done* if you follow these five steps.

1. Know Who You Are and Where You Are

When creating a plan of any kind and implementing it with the aid of a professional advisor, you help yourself and the advisor tremendously by knowing your starting point. So, whether you are twenty-five or fifty-five, the first step toward staying rich for life is to take an inventory of yourself—who you are, where you are, what you want to accomplish. This is where you set the mission for your journey. You may want to write down your thoughts and ideas in black-and-white to review and consider—and possibly change. You might even put them in your BlackBerry or whatever messaging device you frequently use. But writing them down is a much more powerful and effective tool because it gets you to focus and be specific, which is 90 percent of accomplishing any goal. If you now rent, think about whether you want to own a home. Consider the kinds of educational costs you may face for your children. Do you have a dream of traveling to exotic places or being able to take time off from your career to explore a new venture or learn new skills? All of these goals, and many others, require you to plan ahead so you have the funds and the flexibility to make your dreams come true and stay rich for life!

When I meet with first-time retirement planning clients and ask them about their goals, many blurt out, "I just want to avoid paying taxes. I'm paying a fortune now and I want to do anything I can to stop the bleeding!" So I rattle off a bunch of possible solutions: "You can shift this property here, or set up a trust, maybe get some life insurance to help defray your tax bite." And they often respond, "I don't really feel comfortable doing that" or "No, I don't want to do that." And what I learn from this exercise is that even though clients start out saying it's all about cutting taxes, deep down it might not be. It often turns out that they are more concerned about family and legacy issues and making sure their accumulated wealth goes to the people they want it to when they're gone.

Here's another example. I live in New York State, where many clients tell me that what they want to do when they retire is move to Florida. When I ask why, they say, "It's cheaper; there's no state income tax, so our pension income will last longer; and it's warm year-round"—valid reasons all. But within six months of retiring and moving to a warmer, tax-free clime, many return to the frozen, tax-heavy North! The reason they give? They miss their family, or they never see their grandkids. So it turns out that they really did like their life in New York, and who they were and where they wanted to be really wasn't about taxes and the weather at all.

It's the same on the investing side when creating a financial plan. By completing this step, you will find out who you really are (your risk tolerance, for example, or why you own certain assets) and what you're really saving for. Young people, especially, should pay close attention to this step because they have more time to be flexible and make changes. This is important because if there is one thing in life we can count on, it's *change*. It used to be that a person could create a financial plan that would be good for twenty years. But today change seems to come at us every twenty minutes! This step helps you respond to the speed of change in a logical, well-considered way and continue to work toward your specific wealth-building goals by approaching them from different angles.

2. Educate Yourself

Inventorying yourself automatically leads into this next step because as you write down your thoughts and ideas about who you are and where you want to go from a financial planning or retirement planning point of view, you are naturally going to ask where you can get more information on specific topics to enable you to make the right choices. That's where education comes in, and why it is so important. I know for sure that the more informed consumers are about building wealth and preserving it, the better their plans will be for achieving those goals. They will demand more from their professional advisors—financial planners, accountants, attorneys, and insurance agents. There's no question about it. People never put up with hired help that knows less or is less capable than they are.

It's also true that the better informed you are, the less likely you are to fall prey to the strong influence of the most recent conversation you've had about financial matters. Also, you are less likely to blindly accept any advice you get without questioning it. You will be inclined to attend more than one seminar on financial subjects; read more than one book, magazine, or newspaper; and contact more than one potential advisor to decide on the best fit. That's all to the good. It's the same principle you follow when you seek opinions from multiple doctors about a particular medical condition. You do that automatically with something as critical as your physical health. Well, your financial health is just as important. Educate yourself so you can become more actively involved in the process.

3. Avoid Mistakes

Obviously, the better educated you are about saving, investing, and protecting your money, the less likely you are to make a big, costly mistake that could derail your plans or wipe out your nest egg. However, it works the other way, too: Making mistakes is often *how* we learn. But it can be a steep, painful learning curve. I'd rather learn from other people's mistakes, which is why I've included this step.

In the upcoming chapters I'll offer plenty of examples of mistakes people have made in different areas of planning that will read like horror stories. Generally, these mistakes fall into two broad categories: impulsiveness and things that are too good to be true.

An example of a mistake resulting from impulsiveness is a client who tells his broker, "I made such-and-such investment today on a hot tip from my rabbi (or brother-in-law)," or a client who says to me, "I shifted all my money into this tax shelter at the suggestion of my hairdresser (or next-door neighbor)." Don't laugh. Both have happened! A lot of people may give you saving and investing advice during the course of your life, but unless they're professionals who work in the financial services or retirement planning sector, should things go badly, they are neither responsible nor accountable to you for the advice they have given.

As for the other broad category, I've seen some of the smartest, most sophisticated investors and businesspeople lose hundreds of thousands of dollars because they let their minds turn to mush over things that were too good to be true. For example, one of my clients decided to tie up $50,000 of his money for fifteen years by investing in low-income housing in order to get the one-time-only tax break this investment would bring.

"Just think," he exclaimed. "I get a huge tax credit up front!"

"For putting your money in an area where you wouldn't even park your car?" I responded. "Why don't you do this instead? Put the $50,000 in a paper bag, drive to the area you want to invest it in, leave the bag of money in the street, and then come back fifteen years from now and see how much the money grew—because that's what you're doing. Wake up!"

So avoid mistakes. Sure, they can make you smarter, but they can also finish you off.

4. Don't Be Shortsighted

Historians say our country's founders split Congress into two parts precisely so that the new government would never be unduly influenced by the short-term view. The House of Representatives was established first. Its members are elected every two years. This requires them to respond to events swiftly and make decisions expeditiously before the need to campaign for reelection comes around again. To offset the possibility that only bad decisions might result from this situation, the Senate was created to be the more deliberative body. Its members are elected every six years, allowing them to reflect more slowly and take a longer-term view, rather than rushing into rash decisions based on the events of the day. This is how Congress is supposed to work, even if it sometimes doesn't seem that way.

You should approach the process of building and protecting your wealth the Senate way rather than the House way. The objective in creating a financial plan is to achieve the goals you establish. This means sticking to your plan until you get there, not reacting in a knee-jerk way to every new circumstance that happens in a given day or week. You'll never get anywhere with an investment or retirement strategy by continually basing your decisions on short-term events.

5. Take Action in Small, Consistent Steps

I want to emphasize the word *small* in this last of the five fundamental steps to building wealth and keeping it because here it really means "big." Every action you take toward achieving your investing and retirement goals, however minimal that action may seem at the time, produces a big payoff: It gets you closer and leaves you with the feeling of having achieved a victory that will keep you forging ahead.

It's like dieting: Your goal is to lose a hundred pounds. You know you're not going to reach that goal all at once, but you want to avoid that up-and-down, roller-coaster approach to losing weight that's failed you time after time. So you start by tossing out all the junk food in your refrigerator and cabinets. It's a small step, sure, but a *major* one—because with that small step you will have started changing your whole mind-set about losing weight. Next, you go to a gym and get on the treadmill. And you go back again. Pretty soon your mind-set changes even more as you begin to see and explore more opportunities at the gym for getting fit. Your plan begins to take shape. Your path becomes clearer, your decisions better, and the outcome of your efforts more and more positive— just by thinking big but starting out small, and moving ahead deliberatively and gradually.

A Stay Rich Solution

These five steps for staying rich for life flow into each other and work together naturally, cutting to the heart of the many obscure issues connected with building and retaining wealth, and bringing them into sharper focus. Knowing where you're starting from helps narrow your search and leads you to become more informed about each area under consideration. Educating yourself enables you to avoid making mistakes; adopting a long-term view keeps you from jumping at every change in world events or each turn in the financial news and altering your financial plan prematurely. And, finally, taking action in small but consistent steps, rather than taking on the whole challenge in one big swoop, ensures that you will continue to progress toward your wealth-building and wealth protection goals.

I have structured this book to reflect the two halves of the game—the wealth-building, or investment strategies, half (Part II) and the savings protection and wealth preservation half (Part III)— with some key preliminaries introduced in Part I (the warm-up) that apply to both halves of the game and must not be overlooked.

By applying these five steps, or key principles, to the subject considered in each chapter, you will find yourself well on your way to creating a solid financial plan. Once you become involved in creating your plan, the benefits will be enormous:

- You will no longer lose sleep wondering whether your investment strategy is on course.

- You will raise questions about building and retaining wealth that you never thought to ask before and can be sure of getting the right answers from the right sources, especially the professional advisors you will need to effectively implement your plan.

- Finally, but most significantly, you will create a plan that works not for the government, but *for you,* on your own time schedule— a plan that leaves you with more money to enjoy now and more for your retirement, more for your loved ones when you're gone, and more of it tax free.

    And that's how you stay rich for life!

Part I

THE FINANCIAL STORM

"Beginning [in 2008], and for 20 years thereafter, 78 million Americans will become pensioners and medical dependents of the U.S. taxpayer. Federal deficits will grow to unsustainable levels in as little as two decades. At that point, without significant policy changes, federal deficits could reach 10 percent or more of our economy. We're spending more money than we make . . . we're charging it to a credit card . . . *and expecting our grandchildren to pay for it.*"

—David M. Walker, Comptroller General of
the United States, February 2007

Chapter 1

A Y.O.Y.O. ECONOMY—YOU'RE ON YOUR OWN

> When I was young, I used to think that money was the most
> important thing in life; now that I am old, I know it is.
> —Oscar Wilde

Just checking to see whether you read the Introduction, "Five Steps to Staying Rich for Life." If not, go back. I'll wait.

A Nightmare Scenario

You have been putting money away in your 401(k) retirement account on a regular basis since you turned thirty-five in 2005 and began thinking seriously about your financial future. Now it's the year 2040; you are seventy years old and your account has grown to a sizable sum. You have reached the age of eligibility for Social Security benefits, as well. Of course, you will be collecting only half the benefit amount that your baby boomer parents (and *their* parents) did, but, hey, half a loaf is better than none. It helps, right?

Now comes the rude awakening.

All your life, you have believed the conventional "wisdom" that in retirement, as you start withdrawing from your account, you will likely be in a *lower* tax bracket than when you were working. It seems logical, sure.

However, tax increases over the years to pay for out-of-control national deficits and government bailouts, added to the spiraling expense of entitlement programs, plus state and local taxes and the costs of goods and services, have all pushed tax brackets for *everybody* steadily higher. And the result is that, although your tax bracket now may (or may not!) be lower than when you quit working, it is definitely *much higher* than when you started contributing to your 401(k) thirty-five years ago. Yes, you received a tax deduction for every cent you contributed, but the bill for the deductions is now due on every cent you contributed *as well as on every cent it has earned* in interest over those thirty-five years.

Now here's the kicker. Not atypically, your company plan no longer provides health care benefits to retired employees. Most companies eliminated that benefit years ago. So you will have to cover that skyrocketing expense out of your own pocket in whole or in part for the twenty, thirty, or however many years you have left.

The bottom line is this: At the very moment when you need most of the cash you have saved over the years to live comfortably as you had planned, your nest egg is being sucked dry by high taxes and huge expenses, *making retirement, that second home, or your child's education an impossible dream.*

If this nightmare scenario strikes you as far-fetched—a bit too much H. G. Wells or Edgar Allan Poe, with a taste of Ambrose Bierce tossed in for bad measure—consider this. This confluence of evils, what I call the *financial storm,* is not only *going* to hit us, it is hitting us *now*. The precariousness of our financial structure as a result of exploding deficits, multibillion-dollar bailouts, and skyrocketing health care and entitlement costs, coupled with the insecurity of employer-sponsored pension plans when employers experience business downturns or go belly-up, have made it abundantly clear that today's retirement savers must rely on *themselves*. No bailouts for you, since you did everything right! You saved, invested, paid your taxes, and lived within your means. That makes you a good catch for the U.S. tax system, because it imposes a penalty on savers. Our tax-deferred savings are a big, juicy steak for our hungry and insatiable government.

Pension Fund Shortages Create Hard Choices

"Almost half of the states have been under-funding their retirement plans for public workers and may have to choose in the years ahead between their pension obligations and other public programs, according to a comprehensive study released by the Pew Center [a nonpartisan research group that studies public finance and other civic matters]. While some states are managing their costs reasonably well, the center found that others have made serious mistakes and are now cutting education and health programs as they struggle with costs incurred decades ago. Still more states are at risk of being caught in a similar squeeze, the center said, because they are not setting aside enough money now, as their populations age and more public employees approach retirement. Unlike companies, state and local governments are not subject to federal pension laws, which set uniform standards for private industry. If a company skips its required pension contributions, it can be required to pay a big excise tax. No comparable enforcement mechanism exists for states."

—THE NEW YORK TIMES, December 19, 2007

A History of U.S. Tax Rates

You may think that the taxation of your retirement accounts might not be a pressing concern, especially if you have, or intend to have, sizable accumulated assets. After all, the top federal income tax rate is only 35 percent now, and that rate won't be reached until your taxable income hits $372,951 (for 2009). Most people are in lower tax brackets. By the time your children are going to college or you retire and stop earning a living, your income might drop to the point where the federal income tax rate on your withdrawals is only

25 percent or even 15 percent. That could be true, in the very short term. However, tax rates now are at their lowest levels in years. They might be much higher by the time you retire and begin taking taxable distributions from your IRA and other tax-deferred savings.

So Simple, a Caveman Could Do It

"When the 16th Amendment [instituting the federal income tax] was under debate nearly a century ago, the proponents assured Americans that the tax on income would be small and non-intrusive. The amendment was ratified in 1913. Rep. Cordell Hull, who drafted the first income tax, promised that it would apply only to 'the Carnegies, the Vanderbilts, the Morgans and the Rockefellers with their aggregated billions of hoarded wealth.' The original 1040 form in 1914 was so compact, the New York Times *printed it on the front page. There were a grand total of four instruction forms. Now there are 4,000. The opponents of the income tax urged that, at least, there should be a provision to the 16th amendment capping the tax rate at no more than 10 percent. Advocates claimed this was unnecessary because the tax rate would never exceed 10 percent. By 1918, when the government wanted money to fight World War I, the rate was 70 percent."*

—*THE WALL STREET JOURNAL,* April 13, 2008

Let's take a look at the top federal tax rates for each year since the U.S. income tax system began in 1913. Because they are the highest rates, only the very wealthy paid taxes at these rates. History has demonstrated, however, that if Congress came up with rates this high once, it can do so again—and the rates will apply not just to the rich. They will affect many more of us. We need to prepare, because the U.S. government needs more money now than it ever has. Hold on to your wallets!

Notice that for every year but the last during which the baby boomers were born (1946–1964), the top tax rate exceeded 90 percent; in 1964, it dropped to a paltry 77 percent. That was when the boomers were still babies and didn't need all that much from the government. Now this same group has already begun collecting So-

YEAR	TOP FEDERAL INCOME TAX RATE	YEAR	TOP FEDERAL INCOME TAX RATE
1913	7 %	1962	91 %
1914	7 %	1963	91 %
1915	7 %	1964	77 %
1916	15 %	1965	70 %
1917	67 %	1966	70 %
1918	77 %	1967	70 %
1919	73 %	1968	70 %
1920	73 %	1969	70 %
1921	73 %	1970	70 %
1922	58 %	1971	70 %
1923	50 %	1972	70 %
1924	46 %	1973	70 %
1925	25 %	1974	70 %
1926	25 %	1975	70 %
1927	25 %	1976	70 %
1928	25 %	1977	70 %
1929	25 %	1978	70 %
1930	25 %	1979	70 %
1931	25 %	1980	70 %
1932	63 %	1981	70 %
1933	63 %	1982	50 %
1934	63 %	1983	50 %
1935	63 %	1984	50 %
1936	79 %	1985	50 %
1937	79 %	1986	50 %
1938	79 %	1987	38.5 %
1939	79 %	1988	28 %
1940	79 %	1989	28 %
1941	81 %	1990	28 %
1942	88 %	1991	31 %
1943	88 %	1992	31 %
1944	94 %	1993	39.6 %
1945	94 %	1994	39.6 %
1946	91 %	1995	39.6 %
1947	91 %	1996	39.6 %
1948	91 %	1997	39.6 %
1949	91 %	1998	39.6 %
1950	91 %	1999	39.6 %
1951	91 %	2000	39.6 %
1952	92 %	2001	39.1 %
1953	92 %	2002	38.6 %
1954	91 %	2003	35 %
1955	91 %	2004	35 %
1956	91 %	2005	35 %
1957	91 %	2006	35 %
1958	91 %	2007	35 %
1959	91 %	2008	35 %
1960	91 %	2009	35 %
1961	91 %		

cial Security, and 78 million of them, including me, will become, in some form or other, dependents of the government. How high will tax rates have to go to fulfill these needs, promises, and obligations?

> *"History does not repeat itself, but it rhymes."*
> —MARK TWAIN

Not So Ship-Shape

In essence, the S.H.I.P. is going to hit the fan.

- **Social Security** According to the 2008 Annual Report of the Social Security Board of Trustees: "Annual cost will exceed tax income starting in 2017, at which time the annual gap will be covered with cash from redemptions of special obligations of the Treasury that make up the trust fund assets until these assets are exhausted in 2041."

- **Health insurance** Medicare, the federal health insurance program, is in even worse condition, according to the Medicare Board of Trustees. "HI [Hospital Insurance] tax income and other dedicated revenues are expected to fall short of HI expenditures in 2008 and all future years. . . . Closing deficits of this magnitude will require very substantial increases in tax revenues and/or reductions in expenditures," the report states.

- **Income tax** In the future, income taxes are bound to go up. The federal budget deficit for 2008 is projected to top $400 billion. That's with a current surplus in Social Security and a near breakeven in Medicare. This does not include over a trillion dollars in bailout money.

- **Pensions** As of 2007, the federal Pension Benefit Guaranty Corporation (PBGC) already had a $14 billion deficit—that's how much its liabilities from terminated pension plans exceed its assets. And the financial meltdown of 2008 had not yet occurred!

Federal income taxes don't bring in nearly enough to cover the government's expenses. The shortfall is likely to get worse, not better, in the future. Thus, Congress probably will raise income tax rates. Meanwhile, U.S. corporations have a $500 billion deficit in their pension plans. Undoubtedly, some of those billions will wind up as additional obligations of the federal Pension Benefit Guaranty Corporation (PBGC).

Altogether, the federal government has untold billions of present and future liabilities. The most likely way to close the gap is to raise taxes. It's like the airline industry. When they're in bad fiscal shape— as they are now—the airlines find all sorts of ways to get more money from you. These days, if you check a bag, it's an extra $25; if you have to go to the bathroom on the plane, it's an extra $100; if you need the oxygen mask in an emergency, that's $1,000. Okay, maybe it's not really *that* bad . . . yet. But as a frequent flyer, I've come up with a new motto for the airlines: "We're not happy until you're not happy." The delays are so bad these days, that the airlines should stop posting schedules and just post the odds.

But I digress. The point is that income tax rates probably will be higher—perhaps much higher—by the time you begin taking distributions from your IRA. Looking at the history of U.S. tax rates, a 50 percent partner might not be so bad. Instead, however, you can expect Uncle Sam to be a *senior partner.* That means he will get more than you do of every dollar you withdraw from your tax-deferred savings! This does not even include state income taxes, which will also be going up, as states are likewise going broke and need cash to make up their immense budget deficits.

In addition, federal estate taxes are sure to be around for years to come. If you die with a large balance in your IRA, a combination of estate and income tax may claim most of that account.

Indeed, the people Congress prefers to tax are rich people: That's where the money is.

Better yet, Congress is likely to tax dead rich people. They can't vote or contribute to a competitor's campaign.

Best of all, Congress probably will focus on dead rich people's money that never has been taxed. That's money you'll leave in your IRA after your death.

As mentioned, estate and income tax can chew up 70 to 80 percent of your IRA after your death, under current law. Don't be surprised if future tax legislation pushes the norm for double taxation even higher.

All of this means that we are currently in a period of historically low tax rates. Taxwise, most people really don't appreciate how good they have it right now. Since we know what's coming, we need to create a plan to manage the future tax increases.

Because taxes will become the single biggest obstacle to building and preserving wealth, we need to start moving our money from accounts that are forever taxed to accounts that are *never taxed,* so we don't have to share our future savings and earnings with Uncle Sam. Tax-free cash is king.

Tempting Target

You might think that retirement plans will somehow avoid the tax increases to come. After all, Congress won't want to alienate the growing number of seniors, who tend to vote in large numbers.

It may be true that Congress would prefer to spare seniors, but that might not be possible. So much money is sitting in retirement plans that they're the first place politicians will look for tax revenues.

According to the latest report from the Investment Company Institute, total U.S. retirement assets reached $17.4 trillion at the end of the second quarter of 2007. Those assets accounted for almost 40 percent of all household financial assets in the United States.

Of those retirement assets, IRAs and defined contribution plans totaled $9 trillion. Defined contribution plans include 401(k)s and

403(b)s. That's where most of the untaxed dollars are, so you can be sure that those plans will be included in any tax increases. IRAs are the repository of retirement savings. It's where most of the untaxed wealth in this country will end up.

Perhaps some tax breaks will be extended to low-income or low-asset seniors. However, if you have saved a substantial amount in IRAs, 401(k)s, or other such plans, you own your home, and you have a comfortable lifestyle in retirement, you can expect to be asked to turn over a large portion of your retirement funds to the IRS.

As things stand now, the tax system penalizes savers. Those who are most at risk are those who have saved the most, especially those who have saved untaxed dollars.

IRAs, 401(k)s, and the like have never been taxed in most cases. Future tax legislation may well provide for steeper taxes on money withdrawn from those accounts as well as on money left in them to be passed on to beneficiaries. The more you have saved in a retirement plan, the more tax you and your heirs will wind up paying.

If you hope to stay rich for life—to live well in retirement and not just be comfortable or simply get by—you *must take action now to build your own wealth and bring about the retirement future you want.*

U.S. Ruling Backs Benefit Cut at 65 in Retiree Plans

"The Equal Employment Opportunity Commission said Wednesday [December 26, 2007] that employers could reduce or eliminate health benefits for retirees when they turn 65 and become eligible for Medicare. The policy, set forth in a new regulation, allows employers to establish two classes of retirees, with more comprehensive benefits for those under 65 and more limited benefits—or none at all—for those older. The new policy creates an explicit exemption from age-discrimination laws for employers [who] scale back benefits of retirees 65 and over."

—THE NEW YORK TIMES, December 27, 2007

1. Know Who You Are and Where You Are

Wherever you are in the process of building and preserving wealth, the central reality you must face in strategizing is that you're on your own. That's got to be your starting point. The two wells of financial security that workers traditionally draw from—government and business—are both broke. They have nothing left for you, as they might have in the past. You have *only yourself* to rely on now. Maybe you're about to open or already have a 401(k) plan with the company that employs you. Doesn't matter; it's not the company's retirement plan, it's yours. The company has transferred the risk, the reward, and the responsibility of saving for your retirement from its shoulders onto yours, including the *cost,* which you pay for in the form of fees even if you aren't overtly aware of them. Many of these costs are taken right off your investment returns. Lately, most companies are cutting back on contributing matching funds to 401(k) plans. But even if your company contributes some matching funds (which is great!), you're still on your own. All the company has done by making the 401(k) available to you is provide a mechanism for *you* to use to build a nest egg, or not—it's your choice.

It's the same with the government. Yes, you'll pay in to Social Security and at the end, when you retire, you'll get something in return—who knows what amount; that depends on your age when you retire. But if you want a sustainable, good-quality lifestyle in retirement, you're going to need a lot more than that Social Security check to bankroll you. So, even though Social Security is also a plan—albeit a forced savings plan, unlike a 401(k), which is voluntary—you're really on your own here as well if you've got goals and desires larger than just scraping by.

There are no Papa Bear and Mama Bear anymore. Business and government, the two wells to which people typically have gone for financial security, especially when they are the most desperate, have, for all intents and purposes, dried up. So that's your starting point. You're the person in charge, and where you are in this Y.O.Y.O. economy is all by yourself. Now what?

2. Educate Yourself

So now you want to—indeed, you *must*—seek to educate yourself about other things you can do to grow your money and protect it. To be able to accumulate more and to keep more of what you accumulate from being lost to taxes down the road, you will need to find ways to transfer currently taxable money into tax-free accounts, for example. Building wealth that will eventually be taxed does not constitute *real* wealth because a lot of it will be owed back to the government. You need to build *real* wealth—and the key to doing that rests in educating yourself now.

3. Avoid Mistakes

Remember that when you're on your own it's even more important to avoid mistakes, because there will be nobody to blame but yourself.

Building assets means creating a plan for letting them grow and then permitting that to happen, rather than cutting the process short by, say, buying high and selling low while trying to get rich quick. That's a mistake, and it's up to you not to make it.

Similarly, when the time comes to back off a little from the growth angle and shift your focus more toward the income angle, you will only have yourself to blame if you make a costly distribution mistake. The more educated you are about the possibilities for such errors, the greater the likelihood you won't make them.

Even though you are on your own, you still need the guidance of a professional advisor (see Chapter 3) to help you avoid making mistakes. An advisor has the experience and specialized knowledge to steer clear of the numerous tax traps and minefields that can too easily consume your retirement savings. In other words, even though you are on your own, don't try to go it alone.

4. Don't Be Shortsighted

When you're on your own, you have to *think long term* because effective planning isn't—or *shouldn't*—be about doing something once and never thinking about it again. In other words, you can't expect to just sit back and watch that plan unfold. If it is to work and truly be effective, it must continually be revised to reflect whatever major changes come your way throughout your life—getting married, having children (or not), getting divorced, losing or gaining an income in your family, or, perhaps, the premature death of a spouse. Such events don't occur all in one day, week, or month; they unfold over time and thus have an impact on the planning you must do.

Not being shortsighted also means not letting short-term costs get in the way of long-term planning. You need to know the difference between a cost, which is an expense that might bring some immediate gratification but no long-term return, and an investment that will pay off later on—say, in retirement, when you need that return most. For example, buying a big-screen TV is a cost, since it has no long-term return. Yes, you get short-term gratification, but that's not the way to build wealth. You need to focus on the result, not just on what something costs now. This is why so many people wind up making poor financial moves and stay away from things like life insurance (Chapter 12) and Roth IRA conversions (Chapter 8), which require paying money now for a tax-free windfall later. They are letting the up-front cost blur the value of the long-term investment.

Of course, it's good to save money when you can, but not at the risk of losing out on much more later on. Here's an example of what I mean by making a bad decision motivated by the lure of short-term savings or, in this case, *perceived* savings. Some workers keep their money in company 401(k) plans even after they've retired, rather than rolling it over to an IRA, where they would have greater control and better, more flexible distribution and tax options. When I ask them why they don't do a rollover, they explain that it's because they're saving on fees. That's what they believe, but it is absolutely untrue—they simply aren't aware of the fees because the plan is under no obligation to disclose these fees to them. Numerous government bodies are investigating this matter with the aim of putting pressure on 401(k) plans to disclose hidden fees that come right off your investment return.

5. Take Action in Small, Consistent Steps

This step is likewise extremely critical when you're on your own because it encourages you to put money away on a regular basis when no one is forcing you to do so. Saving is a tough discipline to learn. If it were easy, America would be a nation of savers. There's no one to stand over your shoulder and say, "Do this,"—and no one to take care of you if you don't. It's all up to you. Developing the discipline to save, invest, and build a nest egg on your own is the only way to create a huge amount of wealth. You'll be paid back for your efforts—that's for sure.

You don't have to start out by socking away a *lot* of money, either. Real wealth is built little by little over time. This step teaches you to start with small amounts, moving on to larger amounts when you're able to—or remaining with small amounts all the way through if that's your plan, as long as you continue to put money aside on a regular basis. As the saying goes, the tallest of oaks grows from the smallest acorn.

SAMPLE ACTION STEPS

- Participate in a company-sponsored or other qualified retirement plan such as an IRA.
- Put money aside regularly, whatever the amount.
- Think "growth" first and "income protection" second, and learn about both.
- Start now. It is never too early, but it can be too late.

Chapter 2

I'M SO CONFUSED!

ESCHEW OBFUSCATION

—Advice on Bumper Sticker

Noise, Noise, Noise

A money manager friend of mine told me about a client who signed up for an online account in order to be able to monitor his portfolio on the Internet. Within a few days, the client canceled the service. When my friend asked him why, the client said that having so much information available to him at all times of day with the click of a mouse just made him even more nervous and antsy about the market than he already was. It turned out that he was much happier, and much less confused, in a paper-based world.

Stories like that are not uncommon in our Information Age. People often tell me that where their money is concerned, they're *always* anxious—as if it was a natural condition. They're anxious when they're building their nest eggs because some overseas market might hiccup and cause Wall Street to take a tumble. (Hey, this happens!) So as a hedge against potential disaster, they look for guidance. But there are so many investment books to choose from, so many conflicting strategies to consider, and so many tips to sift through from so many financial pundits all over the airwaves and the Internet—in other words, there's so much *noise*—that they feel like burying their heads in the sand like ostriches, hoping their money will take care of itself. The amount of information out there is really overwhelming and can leave you even more confused than when you started out. Not only that, it is all constantly changing at warp speed, constantly making you think that you missed the boat. Does this describe you?

Here's an alternative scenario. Many people who have successfully weathered the various financial storms that inevitably come our way in life have managed to build up their retirement savings, and therefore believe their financial worries are over, suddenly discover by reading my books or attending my seminars that all their money is just on loan to them—because the IRS hasn't taxed it yet! Another blow is the realization that the taxation rules that apply to most retirement plan distributions are so complex, they make your head swim. Furthermore, these rules are riddled with pitfalls, so that making a poor or uninformed decision can have dire—even *catastrophic*—financial consequences.

No wonder you're confused. You're getting hit from *every* side.

When the market is down and you see your savings—whether it's your 401(k), your child's 529 college fund, or your brokerage account—beginning to dwindle, you wonder: "What should I do? Maybe get out of the market? Or sit tight and wait things out?" You are really desperate for *clarity*. That's the thinking during the accumulation half of the game.

If you are already retired and there's a market downturn that causes your IRA or 401(k) to lose money, it becomes even more important to protect what you've got left from excessive taxation on withdrawals. It's enough to make you feel like the kid in the *Home Alone* movies: eyes wide, hands to your cheeks, your mouth screaming, "Ahhhhhhhhh!" You don't know where to turn for help.

In case you're feeling confused—and you probably are, or you wouldn't be reading this chapter—let's apply the five principles to get you unconfused.

Top FAQs . . .

Q: "Ed, I'm so confused! I watch CNBC and all those other business channels every day to stay on top of things, and I still don't know which end is up. What else can I do?"

A: "Turn them off. Always keep in mind that they are for-profit organizations; they demand viewers to boost their ratings and increase their ad revenues. And they get more viewers by delivering information in as dramatic, sexy, and scary a way as possible in order to keep you tuned in as long as possible. Clarity is secondary."

1. Know Who You Are and Where You Are

Ever been in a mall looking for a particular store until your head spins because you can't seem to find it? Here's a tip. Check out a map of the mall before you take a single step. It tells you: "You are here." It shows where you are in relation to the store you're looking for, sparing you a lot of time and confusion, not to mention wear and tear on your feet. In the process of staying rich for life, this same technique for avoiding confusion is called understanding your *time horizon*—where you are in relation to where you want to get.

Say you are in your twenties and just starting to put away money for the down payment on a home and investing in a 401(k) or other retirement account. Experiencing a market downturn (and you can expect to experience more than one in your working lifetime) should not throw you into a complete tailspin. You have many decades until retirement age to recoup any losses you might have suffered, and then some. This is why it is important to start saving early and often: to create a safety net (see Part II, "The First Half of the Game").

Conversely, when you are in your sixties or seventies you want your safety net to already be there for you. At this stage of your life you shouldn't even be thinking about putting more money into the market, no matter what the market is doing. Why? In the event of a downturn, you should be thinking income, not accumulation, and putting your money into safer, more conservative income-producing investments—even into relatively low-earning certificates of deposit (CDs); they're FDIC-insured up to $250,000. Don't put money into the market that's intended for your safety net, or you might face something worse than confusion—that is, the horror of being sixty or seventy and having to work another ten years just to keep yourself afloat (see Part III, "The Winning Half of the Game").

2. Educate Yourself

A friend of mine told me the following story about a famous money maven on television who once worked as a broker selling annuities. Now that she's a pundit, she denounces annuities. So, once annuities were good; now they're bad. What changed? Well, this did: At one time she was selling them; now she isn't. Confusing, isn't it? Well, maybe not so much.

You see, the financial services industry has a stake in fostering confusion because this adds to its mystique of expertise. So the last thing those in the industry, like the money maven I just described, want to do is demystify the financial world. If they did, you wouldn't keep coming back for their help in navigating that world.

The financial world does not exist to keep your head from exploding over money matters but to sell to you and to make a profit. If you, the investor, also happen to make out well, that's great. It's a win-win. But it's not the primary concern of the seller. And the inherent lack of impartiality on the part of the banks and other financial institutions—and yes, the money mavens, too—that are imparting information to you just piles on the confusion, making you question just who you can trust.

One reason my recommendation to clients of life insurance as a sound retirement planning tool and tax-saving strategy (see Chap-

ter 12) is not taken by them as a confusing mixed message is that
they know *I don't sell insurance,* and I never have. Nor do I profit in
any way from the life insurance industry or any of my colleagues
who sell policies by promoting the use of life insurance for this purpose. My clients know they are getting completely unbiased advice
that they can trust, whether they choose to take that advice or not.

So instead of a sponsored event selling a particular point of
view or product, consider taking a noncredit course in financial
planning at your local community college or an area university.
Most of them now offer continuing education courses on money
and finance. Such courses are often very good sources of unbiased
information and advice because they are taught by academics or
other professionals with no vested interest in selling a product or
service.

In addition to being a source of *noise* (investing advice you
should tune out), the Internet also is a tremendous source for basic
information about investing. It can be an excellent educational tool in
this subject, if you know where to look. Here are some websites I
know about and that advisors have recommended to me as resources
for learning about investing and avoiding conflicting advice:

- **www.aarp.org** You don't have to be over fifty and approaching
  retirement to tap into this site sponsored by the American Association of Retired Persons (AARP). It's a comprehensive source
  for good, basic information about investing. For example, the
  difference between investing and saving can be confusing. Investing means using income to buy something with the prospect
  that it will earn more income and increase in value over time;
  saving means to hold on to income. This site employs simple, direct, user-friendly language to discuss fundamentals such as *basic
  investing principles, how to allocate your money to meet your goals,
  saving for college,* and *the impact of investment fees,* as well as explaining *cash equivalents, bonds, stocks, mutual funds, exchange-
  traded funds, foreign fund investing, socially responsible investing,*
  and *variable annuities.*

- **www.morningstar.com** Although Morningstar is fundamentally a source of advice for veteran investors and the advisors who serve them, it also provides a lot of basic knowledge about the investing world for beginners. And it puts this information in one easy-to-find and easy-to-use space on its site. Just click the Learning Center link and navigate your way through tutorials on everything from explaining what constitutes a capital gain to the different ways an investment can make you money.

- **www.smartaboutmoney.org** Operated by the National Endowment for Financial Education, this site is designed to help you learn the basics about money, providing free, unbiased information on virtually every topic beginners and even seasoned veterans need to understand. It also lists many courses and workshops on financial learning that are offered around the country.

How much will you have to learn to feel sufficiently educated and less confused about investing and money-related issues? You should reach a point at which you feel comfortable questioning your bank or other financial institution—and what the pundits are saying—about a particular investment vehicle or strategy they're touting, and whether it is truly right for *you*.

"It's not really all that difficult," an investment advisor tells me about what it takes to reach that point. "Understanding money simply boils down to knowing that it's not what you gross but what you net that counts," he says. "You want to be able to enjoy a certain standard of living for yourself and your family during your working years and then be able to maintain that standard of living, or close to it, in your retirement years. Just *existing* is what terrifies—that you will have money but can't take those vacations you've always dreamed of with your wife, or give to your children the way you want to, because you're fearful you may need that money for a rainy day. It's fear of not having enough money in retirement that keeps people awake at night or from enjoying their retirement years. So, the bottom line is this: It's always the net—what you *keep*—that counts."

3. Avoid Mistakes

The most common mistake people make about investing, my advisor friends insist, is trying to pick out the "hot dot"—that is, the current investment fad—and chasing it. Because it's "what you keep that counts," chasing the hot dot can lead to financial catastrophe. It's a lot more difficult to bounce back from a loss than it is to avoid that loss in the first place.

"In other words, it isn't nearly as hard going from $8,000 to $14,000 as it is going from $14,000 down to $8,000 then back up again to $14,000," a colleague explains. "You will need an exponential return to overcome that loss, so keep a clear head by never putting too much risk on a gain." (See Chapter 7 for more on this and other guidelines for confusion-free investing.)

Here's another big mistake to refrain from making. Wherever you may be along your time horizon—whether you are in your twenties and just starting to save or in your fifties and nearing retirement—let's say you've done everything this book says to do to set yourself up to stay rich for life. You feel great because you've completed all your due diligence, you've mapped out an action plan, and you've put together that ace team of advisors (discussed in Chapters 3, 4, 5, and 12) to implement your plans effectively. Then the day comes to start dipping into your nest egg or passing it on to your chosen heirs tax free and, *bang!,* the bottom falls out of everything because one or more of your accounts can't be located. Or there's been a birth, a death, a marriage, or a divorce that affects your intentions, but you haven't updated your financial plan to reflect those life changes. Or neither you nor anybody else can find the important documentation that affects how your money will be passed on and to whom. You want confusion? Here it comes—in bucket loads!

I cannot tell you how often something like this happens. When it comes to retirement planning—from accumulation of wealth through distribution of that wealth—the phrase *once is not enough* truly applies. You may have taken definite action to develop a comprehensive financial plan, or someone has taken it for you, but you can't just sit back and consider the job done. If you never reexamine or consider those actions again, you'll likely be in for a shock. It used to be that when I prepared an estate plan with a client it would be valid for twenty years. Now it doesn't last twenty minutes, because of tax law changes, market volatility, and economic conditions and family situations that are constantly changing. As the old saying goes, "The only constant is change." You must anticipate changes and create plans that are fluid and flexible enough to accommodate them. Don't make the mistake of thinking that once you've completed your plan (a big victory in itself), your work is done. It isn't. Your plan is always subject to change.

For example, a client says to me, "My financial advisor and I went over everything with my accountant and estate planning attorney, and it's all taken care of."

"When was that?" I ask.

"Oh, maybe ten years ago," the client responds, pleased to have been so far ahead of the curve.

Then I ask, "Where's the beneficiary form for your retirement account?"

"Oh, I'm sure the bank has it" is the answer. And then, after some digging, we find that this single most critical document in the client's estate plan for preserving and passing on his retirement assets is nowhere to be found by anyone. Why not? As a result of recent financial crises, a lot of financial institutions have gone belly up, merged with other banks, or been acquired by another financial institution—including my client's. And amid the turmoil, the last thing anybody at the embattled bank was thinking about was my client's beneficiary form. So I doubted that anybody had called him to say, "We've just been taken over by another company, but I've got your beneficiary form in my hand and am taking it to the new bank with me."

Let's say that the client's new bank does have the beneficiary form, but the client has not kept it up-to-date to reflect his current wishes resulting from some change in his life circumstances. Thus, if he gets hit by a bus that day, his hard-earned savings will go to his ex, from whom he was divorced five years previously, instead of to his current spouse as he had wished. There'll be no big send-off for him, I'll bet.

And there is this final mistake to avoid. Staying rich for life is not a one-man-band, do-it-yourself process, whether it's the saving and investing or the preserving side of building wealth. No matter how well you have educated yourself about all the angles involved, at some point you will need professional guidance to keep your head from spinning as a result of all the complex strategies, rules, and regulations that no layperson could possibly absorb. Even the savviest experts have to work hard to keep up with this stuff—but it's their business to do so. You are *not* in that business. You will need advisors with specialized knowledge in all aspects of wealth building, from investing to withdrawing and leaving that wealth to your heirs. The role of these advisors is to prevent you from doing something wrong or, worse, doing *nothing*—which could be fatal to your wealth-building and retirement-planning goals. Trying to be your own all-purpose guru on financial matters is a crucial mistake to avoid.

4. Don't Be Shortsighted

Top FAQs . . .

Q: "Ed, I'm so confused. You keep talking about IRA savings. But I don't save in an IRA. I have a 401(k), and my wife works for the state and has a 403(b) retirement account. So, what should we be doing?"

A: "The same. Regardless of whether the stocks, bonds, cash, mutual funds, or whatever your investment portfolio consists of are held in a 401(k) or any other type of qualified retirement account, you will generally end up transferring the accumulated worth into an IRA when you start taking distributions. Unless, of course, you take a lump-sum distribution from your employer at retirement and blow it all on a trip to Capistrano."

5. Take Action in Small, Consistent Steps

As the saying goes, a journey of a thousand miles begins with a single step. Recognize that staying rich for life is a long-term commitment. This discipline is key to avoid being overwhelmed and confused by the process. Everything will be fine the minute you start making even a small dent in what may at first seem to be a daunting task.

As you dip your toe into the ocean that is creating, implementing, and monitoring your wealth-building and savings plans, you will find that addressing one issue uncovers another that needs addressing, then another, and another, and so on down the line. Nothing is going to happen overnight—and it's *good* that it doesn't! That would be too much information to absorb and process at once—like opening a fire hydrant for a glass of water and being hit with a gusher. As you take each little step, a light goes on. With each additional step, another light goes on, till your path is lit like an airstrip at night, guiding an airplane to a safe landing. And you will begin to feel better, knowing that you are gradually covering all the issues, concerns, and abstract details that are now making you feel so confused.

SAMPLE ACTION STEPS

- Identify and understand your time horizon.
- Learn the basics about managing money.
- Seek unbiased information and assistance.
- Periodically review and update your key planning documentation.
- Store your key plan documents in a safe place, easily accessible to yourself and your heirs.

Chapter 3

PICKING THE *RIGHT* FINANCIAL ADVISOR FOR *YOU*

"The only reason a great many American families don't own an elephant is that they have never been offered an elephant for a dollar down and easy weekly payments."

—*Mad* magazine

Too Much to Absorb

It goes without saying that staying truly healthy requires more than just eating an apple every day. You can still become ill and require medical attention—or, the older you get, preventive medicine such as a flu shot. In other words, you can't expect to go through life without ever needing a doctor. And depending on what the medical issue is, you will want that doctor to be the best there is *for you* in that particular area.

So it is with saving, investing, and retirement planning. There is just too much to keep up with for you to try to manage it all yourself. Along the way you will develop different needs that require different types and levels of professional savvy to keep you healthy and on course with your changing financial strategies and goals.

The first level of expertise you will need is that provided by a professional financial advisor, also known as an *asset manager* (and sometimes called by other names, depending on how well or poorly the advisor performs). Many advisors are very capable of leading you through the first half of the game—the accumulation half. Financial planners and investment advisors generally are familiar with the concepts of diversification and asset allocation. They know the importance of holding down investment costs. Many advisors recommend specific stocks, bonds, or funds, with some success. They may work for large financial institutions with capable research staffs. So there's a good chance that your advisor will get you into the locker room in good shape at halftime. However, most advisors will be little or no help to you in the third and fourth quarters of the game. Few advisors are knowledgeable about retirement plan distributions or have any training in minimizing the tax on these distributions. They are *salespeople*, not really financial advisors, and they don't want to take any time away from selling; in fact, they often tell me that straight out.

For example, a young broker came into my office last year to do his taxes. He told me he had just begun working at a big national brokerage firm. I congratulated him and said he was in a great position to help so many people who need it, especially now, in this Y.O.Y.O. economy, and I recommended that if he really wanted his clients to be successful he should learn as much as he could about the second half of the wealth stockpiling game: retirement distribution planning. Then I showed him a brochure for an upcoming two-day intensive training program my company was putting together on that subject. "Learning this is what will set you apart from most other people in your field," I said. He looked the brochure over quickly, then shook his head and replied, "I don't need to know any of this. At our brokerage firm, they tell us we only need to know how to sell." That's when I knew I had just a salesperson and not a real planner in front of me. And there was nothing I could do or say to alter his mind-set. A year later, his firm was one of those decimated by the 2008 financial crisis, and he was out of a job. That's why you don't want just salespeople for advisors; they're always the first to go when the market tanks. And where does that leave you?

Not wanting to know is even worse than just plain ignorance. And many brokerage firms *don't* want to know. They just want to sell. Well, that's not good enough for you. For years I have listened to horror stories from clients about how they lost entire chunks of their retirement savings not to the market but to bad advice from salespeople posing as financial planners and advisors. That is why I have been on a mission to match consumers like you to competent, educated advisors.

To give you an idea how deep this problem is, I publish an eight-page monthly newsletter for advisors, CPAs, and attorneys called *Ed Slott's IRA Advisor.* In 2009, we will mark our twelfth year in print. When I first began publishing this newsletter people would say to me, "Ed, how are you going to write eight pages a month about how to take money out of an IRA or company plan?" Well, twelve years later we still haven't run out of material. It's still a challenge getting all the information on new tax laws, cases, rulings, and ever-changing planning strategies into each issue. Subscribers often tell me this information has saved their clients a fortune in taxes and has prevented them from making embarrassing and costly mistakes. Currently there are probably more than one million professional financial advisors out there, including financial planners, CPAs, and attorneys, yet only about four thousand of them invest in getting this information from me, much of which is not readily available to them or their companies without investing tens of thousands of dollars in tax services, as I do. So if they are not willing to spend $125 a year for a subscription to my newsletter to find out what is going on in this constantly evolving field, it is even less likely that they are spending thousands more on extensive educational programs and tax services.

Perhaps I am being harsh here, but not without cause. Chances are, your current advisor is among those I'm describing and, therefore, not fully up to the task of serving *all* your planning needs. I don't want you and your family to find this out too late, after the damage has already been done.

As I've written, the big difference is education. You need an advisor who invests in his or her own education. In fact, after reading this book (and my others!), you might know more about the subject than most advisors you meet. Nevertheless, you shouldn't try to handle your financial and retirement planning entirely on your own.

Like a surgeon about to operate on the brain, you should know all you can about how to proceed, but you don't want to try the procedure on yourself. You should seek out an advisor with experience and expertise in this vital subject (yes, there are some).

There is one group of advisors that I know has made the commitment to continuing education in the distribution and taxation of retirement accounts. Why? Because they belong to Ed Slott's Elite IRA Advisor Group,™ an advanced learning program for select advisors who believe in investing in their own professional education so they can do the best overall job for their clients. They are listed on my website at www.irahelp.com, and there are hundreds of them all over the country. Go to the website and you will probably find one in your area.*

Beware of the glossy brochures and of advisors, especially those at big brokerage firms and banks, who say they get their training and education "in-house." That kind of training and education is meaningless to you in terms of the big picture because it tends to focus only on how to sell you products and services. That's fine, but it's not enough to help you create a well-thought-out financial plan.

A savvy advisor will help you avoid a major error that many people make with their retirement savings: admiration. That is, they just sit there and watch it grow, with no consideration given to what can happen when they start taking withdrawals. If you just sit there and admire it, sure, you'll wind up with a large nest egg—and a large income tax bill when the money comes back out. There may be estate tax, too, when you die, and still more income taxes for your beneficiaries.

So let's begin by applying the five steps for staying rich for life to picking the right advisor *for you*.

---

* NOTE: My company provides these advisors with educational materials on a year-round basis so they are constantly kept up-to-date. I do not receive any compensation on stocks, bonds, funds of any kind, annuities, or life insurance products sold by these advisors, nor do I sell these products myself.

1. Know Who You Are and Where You Are

Keeping to our medical analogy, if you go to a doctor and can't explain your symptoms or pinpoint the source of your pain, how can you expect the doctor to be of much help to you? Similarly, if you can't articulate where you currently stand financially—that is, what you own and why—and express where you want to go, no financial advisor worth his or her salt will be able to provide you with a real solution for your needs. That is because you will not have given the advisor enough of a picture of you as an individual to be able to suggest anything but a cookie-cutter, one-size-fits-all investing approach, which is often no answer at all. But if you can truly articulate where you are right now and how you got there, and be realistic about where you want to be in ten, twenty, thirty, forty, fifty, or however many years, the advisor can develop a clear picture of your *investor personality*—the foundation he or she will need to help tailor a wealth-building investment portfolio for you.

"If someone says to me, 'If my assets get cut in half in a market downturn, not only are my hopes and dreams dashed, but I'm in serious trouble of never being able to retire,' or if another says to me, 'If things were to go bad in the market, I know I couldn't handle staying the course to ride things out,' I have a pretty good idea of where they are coming from emotionally insofar as their approach to money is concerned," a top-flight advisor says.

"Unfortunately," this advisor continues, "people have this belief that investing is the great ATM in the sky, and a dollar today is going to be worth four dollars some day in the future absolutely *guaranteed*. Well, that's not really the case. Everybody likes market volatility on the upside. That's the easy part; nobody's ever going to complain about that. It's when market volatility starts to go against you where your real investor personality comes through. It's often then that I see who are the really calm, cool, and collected customers, and who should maybe never have been invested the way they are to begin with. So if you can truly articulate what your 'pain threshold' is, that will make the advisor's life a lot easier in terms of finding the correct solution for you."

How do you become knowledgeable (and self-aware) enough to feel comfortable interviewing and opening up to a candidate to be your financial advisor? Well, first some information gathering is in order.

2. Educate Yourself

Investment advisors admit the same thing about evaluating their prospective clients that I do about mine on the planning and distribution end. At the very least you must be able to communicate with us at some level of experience and expertise. Where financial advisors are concerned, you should at least have absorbed enough information so that you can be actively involved in your own investment planning. You should know enough to be able to ask the advisor, "Why is this investment product or this solution appropriate for me? What are the pros and cons, the upsides and the downsides?" And if the advisor is unable to answer your question quickly and clearly and gives you a convoluted response, you will know immediately that not only is that advisor not right for you, but probably neither is the product or solution.

Education is paramount. I'm not saying that you have to know all the gory details, but you have to know enough to ask key questions and be able to verify that your advisor knows the answers to those questions, which will tell you whether you have the right advisor. Simply understanding general concepts will help you make better decisions. There is no question that informed consumers always end up with better-educated advisors because the average consumer is not going to stand for an advisor who knows less than the consumer does. For example, did you ever go to make a major purchase—say, a big appliance or a car—and within five seconds of talking to the salesperson you realize, "Hey, *I* know more than this guy!" This is a major purchase. You're spending a lot of money. How does that realization make you feel?

Handling your life savings is equivalent to making a major purchase—*really major*—and because there may be no do-overs or second chances, you want to work with somebody who knows more than you do. If you are buying a car, for example, you don't want to be told that the brakes have to be checked from time to time—that's simplistic. Even people who don't drive know that!

I call this the *crossover point*—the point at which you know as much or more than the salesperson. If you reach this point with a financial advisor, one of two things is likely to happen. Either you will find an advisor who is better educated about preserving your wealth as well as building it, and will do a better job for you in *both* areas, or the government will come in with its own plan for preserving your wealth—meaning, it will scoop up all of your assets that it can for itself.

Obviously, the more education you have about money and investing, the more you will be drawn to advisors who know more than you do. If you aren't at least curious, you may end up with one who will provide a plan, but it won't necessarily be the plan that will make you the most money or enable you to keep most of it. Your lack of curiosity will be revealed in your net worth, which will be lower. You will have settled for an advisor who might know more than you do but probably doesn't know that much, and because you were okay with that, you end up in LOJI—the land of joint ignorance.

FYI . . .

When I train financial advisors in retirement planning and wealth distribution issues, I tell them that if they want to be successful, they have to do the best job they can for their clients. The only way to do the best job is to know as much as they can about the subject, to truly be experts on retirement tax rules, retirement plan withdrawals, tax management, and so on. That's how an individual advisor can rise above his or her competitors. The sad truth is that although most financial advisors are reasonably well educated about investing to build wealth, they are *not* so well educated about preserving and protecting that wealth. And when that is the case, the losers are their clients.

What to Know

Investing, like retirement planning, is a *process,* not an event. You know the old saying about learning how to ride a bike: You can't do it at a seminar. You've got to climb on, plant your feet squarely on the pedals, and give it a go—and keep going until you can stay up and feel comfortable and secure in your ability to ride. It's the same with building a portfolio. You have to get your feet wet in order to have an idea of the depth you're swimming in.

Most everybody knows what a share of stock is, but in today's investing world, shares of stock are not all plain vanilla. There are a lot of investment choices and products out there. Some are very good, and some are not so good. You need to educate yourself about the basics—the nuts-and-bolts concepts, the jargon—just to be able to start asking the right questions, which is integral to any education process.

It's a harsh truth that many advisors will not take on clients with limited investing backgrounds and little or no accumulated assets. This is not because they are *all* coldhearted and money hungry. It's because they are businesspeople who have only so many hours in the day and so many resources to go around; therefore, they can't afford to take a lot of time away from their veteran clients—the people who pay the bills—to spend on newcomers, even if they might like to. Asset management is a business, after all.

So if you have little knowledge of and experience at dabbling in the investment world because you are just starting to focus on building your wealth, you are already in a tough spot for picking an advisor. Investors who have accumulated at least some level of wealth will always have more options open to them in terms of both investment vehicles and high-caliber financial advice than someone who is just starting out. Conversely, beginning investors with fewer assets to work with and less experience to draw on will have fewer choices available than a veteran with a big portfolio, and getting a leg up may prove to be less daunting and confusing precisely because they don't have a world of options open to them.

Many financial advisors I know recommend that after bringing yourself up to speed on the fundamentals (see Chapter 2 for some excellent online resources for learning the basic terms and tools of investing), beginners should start out in the mutual fund world (see Chapter 7, "Investment Strategies for Now and Later"). Then, as their assets grow, they can move up the scale a little bit each time, increasing their access to the best products and the best financial advisors as they go.

What to Look For

Often, the best financial advisors are those with a broader scope, who are active in their local, not just national, financial planning organizations, and who are engaged in a wide range of activities in their communities. So be sure to ask for an advisor's résumé.

Make advisors take a few minutes to tell you about themselves. Believe me, none will say no. But you know where to go if one does—out the door. It's just human nature for people to want to talk about themselves, especially if they have a solid story to tell. And while you are listening, look around the office. It may tell you a lot about who the advisor is and whether there is much chance of a meeting of minds between you. For example, if you're a family guy but don't see any pictures of a wife and kids adorning the desk or office walls, but you do see large, gaudy posters of racing cars, you are going to learn something about what you may or may not have in common. Some degree of shared interests is *always* important in building any kind of relationship, professional or private.

Something else to inquire about when interviewing financial advisors is how much "bench strength" they have. Just as you turn to a financial advisor for the answers he or she can offer you, advisors should have resources to which they can turn for the answers they need to complex questions outside their own areas of expertise. Investing and retirement planning are never just a one-person operation. There are a lot of people behind the scenes on whom advisors can and should be able to draw for the missing pieces needed to complete a particular client's portfolio-planning puzzle.

For example, even though the elite and master teams of IRA advisors who are members of Ed Slott's Elite IRA Advisor Group consider themselves pretty savvy about the retirement and distribution side of staying rich for life, they still sometimes call me or my staff for additional information—just as I have called on them for their knowledge and insights into the wealth-building side of the equation for this book.

No single advisor is in possession of *all* the answers about growing and preserving wealth. And any who boast that they are—who claim they don't require bench strength—are not to be believed, let alone trusted. Very often it is the financial advisor who serves as the point person for assembling the right mix of specialists—attorneys for estate planning, CPAs for tax issues—to solve your particular problem. So press the issue. Ask advisors to give you some examples of their most complex investing or retirement planning client cases and whose help they were able to draw on to resolve different issues. They do not have to share proprietary or confidential information or the names of the clients and resources involved, nor would you expect them to. You're just trying to get a big-picture view of the advisor's professional savvy, versatility, and strength.

And while you're in the process of discovering the depth and quality (or lack thereof) of an advisor's bench strength, ask for some real-life examples of that advisor's own work with clients and the results that were achieved.

"Very few prospective clients do this," a member of my own support team of asset managers informs me. "They should ask to see some actual investor portfolios. Not the names, but how the portfolios are set up, where did the assets come from, and how did they perform for the investor—for example, someone who is X-years-old with X amount of money to work with. If the advisor is any good, he or she is going to have a lot of accounts and a lot of assets under management, and be able to give you some diverse examples. It is likely the advisor will even have someone like you under management already—let's say you're fifty years old with close to a million dollars and you want to retire in ten years. Get the advisor to show you what the performance scenario of someone in similar shoes looks like. And ask for the *real* performance, not the back-tested, hypothetical, or incubator performance some advisors will pull out in the form of pie charts, but the *real stuff.* Sharing that is completely allowed, just no personal client information."

You should also ask advisors how often they contact their clients and what's appropriate in terms of frequency for you to contact them, my colleague adds. "You don't want to be a pain, but you also don't want to be forgotten about," he says. "That can happen, especially in this financial environment, where margins have compressed. I make less money today managing a client's assets than I did fifteen years ago, requiring me to have more clients. The problem is that a lot of advisors in the same circumstances will start warehousing their clients. That is, they will give you cookie-cutter strategy A, B, or C, put you into that model, then stick you on the shelf. And hopefully everything will work out. So, it's in your best interest to find out how many client relationships the advisors you are considering have, and to get them to walk you through their day."

Finally, if you are older and want to connect with a financial advisor for the specific purpose of helping you create an estate plan (see Chapter 13) for passing your wealth on to your heirs, here's what an advisor who specializes in estate planning recommends that you ask. "The first thing I would want to know from the advisors is if they have knowledge of taxation, especially the death [i.e., estate] taxes. I would want to know how they go about keeping up with changes in the tax code in this area. Also, what percentage of their business is doing estate planning? If they do less than 10 percent, stay away from them. They should be doing 30 to 40 percent of their business in that type of planning. Ask what attorneys they work with, and if they're not working with quality estate planning attorneys, stay away—because financial advisors who do estate planning and estate tax attorneys work together as a tightly knit team. Find out if they have knowledge of insurance as a tool for keeping an estate from being decimated by taxes. Are they up to speed on trusts, which can be used for similar purposes? Do they have a trust in their own estate plan? Do they have irrevocable or revocable trusts? Speaking as a financial advisor myself, these are some of the questions *I* would be asking of any advisor I'm considering, especially in the area of estates. The more information you can gather, the surer your chances of picking the one who is truly right for *you*."

Where to Look

In many ways, choosing a financial advisor who is right for you is like picking the right contractor to do some major improvements on your home. You're probably not just going to grab the phone book and blindly pick a name. You start out by asking for references from friends or associates who have had similar work done and were pleased with the results. This is also where you should start when you choose a financial advisor.

Believe it or not, as gargantuan as the financial services world may seem (and as Madison Avenue-ish as it may present itself), it's still a very down-home, local-oriented community that operates largely by word of mouth. Even though many financial advisors have clients all over the country, or even the world, most of their customers are in their own backyards. This is because most investors want to be able to go in on at least a semiregular basis and actually see and have some personal interaction with the men and women who are managing the single largest asset they own—their retirement savings. You should want and expect this, too. So always begin locally by asking around for referrals from friends, business colleagues, and so on, to get you pointed in the right direction. But when asking for referrals, let the buyer beware—an advisor who was touted by a friend who is now on food stamps can be a strong indicator that you should look elsewhere.

Professional organizations are another excellent source for finding a financial advisor because they offer considerable background information about all listed members, including their professional designations and credentials, which are important indicators in assessing an advisor's degree of experience and credibility.

FYI . . .

A note about professional designations: It is always best to choose to work with advisors who have a professional designation because this means they are subject to regulation and oversight. Being licensed advisors, they are in jeopardy of losing their licenses and their livelihood if they fail to live up to the standards set by the licensing organization. That being said, however, having a professional designation does not necessarily mean the advisor has any expertise in retirement distribution planning. That needs to be *your* requirement of *any* advisor (financial, legal, or tax) with whom you work, if you truly want to stay rich for life.

Here are what I consider to be some of the best websites for unbiased information about financial advisors all across the country and how to reach them:

- **www.finra.org** Financial Industry Regulatory Authority (FINRA) is the largest independent regulator for all securities firms doing business in the United States. As a not-for-profit financial resource, FINRA offers unbiased information on a full range of issues that affect your money and investments, as well as background on individual planners and brokers, and other resources for learning about investing. It's motto is "Education, not opinions."

- **www.fpanet.org** The Financial Planning Association (FPA) provides the names and backgrounds of thousands of member certified financial planning (CFP) professionals around the country. The CFP designation is significant because it indicates that an individual has successfully completed the Certified Financial Planner Board of Standards initial and ongoing certification requirements and adheres to the FPA's code of ethics.

- **www.imca.org** Investment Management Consultants Association (IMCA) sets the standards and practices for the investment management consulting profession and provides investment consultants with the credentials and tools required to best serve their clients. The cornerstone of IMCA is the Certified Investment Management Analyst (CIMA) designation, which indicates that the designee has at least three years of broad experience in the field of investment management, has passed an extensive background check, and has completed IMCA's two-step, graduate-level program of study. The site lists IMCA's more than 5,500 CIMA designees and contact information.

- **www.irahelp.com** This is my own site. It lists the names and contact information for every financial planner and asset manager in the country who belongs to either Ed Slott's Elite IRA Advisor Group or Ed Slott's Master Elite IRA Advisor Group. This means they have the tools and training materials they need to stay up-to-date on all the fine points of the second half of the savings and investing game: retirement plan distribution, protection, and preservation—the half that some financial advisors often fall down on.

FYI . . .

I came across some advice one time that went something like this: "Focus on your strengths and hire out your weaknesses." That's what successful people do. And it's what you should do, too—both in deciding how to use your financial advisor and in determining whether that advisor is the right one for you.

3. Avoid Mistakes

The biggest mistake investors of any age make when selecting a financial advisor is being too lazy, industry insiders tell me. They will base their decision on an advertisement they saw on television, a press release about the advisor in the business section of the local newspaper, or the advisor's website, without doing any further research. The thinking goes that this person must be successful because he advertises, that person must be highly regarded because she's gotten a write-up in the paper, or the other person must be really tuned in to technology and all the new investment products and methods out there because he or she has a website. And they convince themselves that this or that person must automatically be right for them.

A related mistake that investors make out of laziness is staying with a financial advisor long after the relationship has proved that it's not working.

"It's not hard, it really isn't, to do some degree of due diligence," says one advisor, who has his own practice within a much larger worldwide asset management firm. "With what's on the Internet today, you can find almost anything you need to about anybody in this business. For example, go to www.FINRA.org and it will show you whether a prospective advisor/broker has or ever has had any regulatory or other investing-related lawsuit filed against him or her, and things of that nature. FINRA oversees nearly 5,000 brokerage firms, about 173,000 branch offices, and approximately 677,000 registered securities representatives. It is one of the best sources for finding out whether the advisors you're considering are being investigated by the state or the Securities and Exchange Commission (SEC), or whether they have a solid reputation as being sound, responsible practitioners of their craft. That's one good starting point to avoid mistakes."

Staying with the wrong advisor until it's too late is a mistake investors make all the time, top financial advisors tell me. As one advisor commented, "People come in here after going it alone for too long, or after having gone with someone who put them in flavor X, Y, or Z so that their portfolios are not right for them or even in the ballpark, and it doesn't matter; they're stuck. They're down substantially, and it's too late. The math is easy. If you lose 50 percent of your assets, you need to double that to get back to the break-even point. So get involved early, and stay involved—don't pull an 'I don't want to know, just do the right thing for me.' It's your money, after all."

Whether you are saving for retirement in a 401(k), a 457, or a 403(b) plan, most of that money is eventually going to wind up in your own personal retirement account when you actually do retire and roll the money over into an IRA or Roth IRA. So make sure your advisor does not make mistakes with those accounts, because they are subject to very complex tax rules. You need to educate yourself so that you will know what your advisor is doing (or, perhaps, not doing) to avoid making horrible mistakes.

Having a top-notch advisor is so important. I have seen people save for fifty years and then make a mistake when they go to take funds out of their account, especially with tax-deferred money, which is strangled by a labyrinth of rules and regulations about withdrawals. A mistake can cost you up to 60 percent of your retirement savings in an instant. Fortunes have been lost in seconds because of mistakes made by advisors who gave the investors poor advice or simply by handing off an inherited account improperly. Recently I was with a client I hadn't seen in ten years—he finally came back in for a review. He has designated his children as the beneficiaries of his $561,000 IRA. I asked him whether, based on the direction I had given him at our last meeting, his advisor had set him up properly for the eventual handoff and whether his kids knew what to do when they inherited to avoid being taxed on their bequest all in one shot. He answered yes, but the more I probed him, the more I could see that he was set up all right—set up for a fall, and so were his kids! This is why you need an advisor with specialized knowledge. Then you must follow the advisor's recommendations for getting the most, not the least, from our financial system.

4. Don't Be Shortsighted

Unless you are elderly and your life expectancy is quite short, money issues are going to be a big part of your life for a long time.

The process of building wealth, by its nature, virtually requires you to take a long-term perspective on saving and investing for your future. That long-term view includes working with an advisor. You don't necessarily stay with someone forever, but if the relationship is succeeding—well, "if it ain't broke, don't fix it." After all, nothing succeeds like success. Nevertheless, the long-term view demands that when deciding whether an advisor is right for you, you raise the question of what happens to you should something happen to the advisor.

For example, if the advisor you are considering is elderly, what contingency plans does the person have in place for managing your assets in the event of his or her death or incapacity? Whether young or old, solo practitioners in particular bring along some risk in this area because if something happens to them, their clients might be left out in the cold with no one to step in and assume the advisor's responsibilities. This makes it all the more important that financial advisors have other resources for the practice to rely on, a support team, and a succession plan (see Chapter 5) in place, so client accounts will continue to be managed as smoothly and effectively as before.

Remember, what happens to your advisor and you in the short term affects what happens to you, your money, and your plans for yourself, your family, and your heirs in the long term.

5. Take Action in Small, Consistent Steps

They had to cancel the Procrastinator's Conference in Orlando this year. Do you know why? They put it off too long, and the hotel was completely booked. It's an old joke, but a telling one.

There is no need to know who you are and where you are, no reason to educate yourself or learn about the mistakes you should avoid making, no need to take a long-term view (or any view, for that matter) when picking a financial advisor, if you don't take action. So step number five is, perhaps, the most important.

Everybody believes they have all the time in the world. But unless you've been gifted (or cursed) with a talent for prophecy, you have no way of knowing how much more time you have left on earth, so you have no control over that. But you *do* have control over this second, this minute, and the hours of time you have *today.*

SAMPLE ACTION STEPS

- Start local before expanding your search.
- Know the tools and terms of investing and retirement planning.
- Know what you own and why you own it.
- Understand and articulate your "pain threshold."
- Be curious and ask questions.
- Get client stories and *real* results.
- Be actively involved in your own financial planning.

Chapter 4

PICKING THE *RIGHT* ACCOUNTANT FOR *YOU*

If Stupidity got us into this mess,
then why can't it get us out?
—Will Rogers

It's Human Nature

In all my years as a certified public accountant (CPA), very rarely has somebody come to me and said, "Ed, I just want to do some proactive planning about taxes—you know, to check that things are okay." It's usually a major event that triggers the visit.

For example, a person might have a major health issue—be terminally ill and want to put his or her financial house in order. Another big event, especially for people with retirement accounts, is when their seventieth birthday approaches and they know that six months later they must start withdrawing from their retirement accounts according to the IRS's age requirement for taking distributions. And so they figure they better start planning now for how to go about doing this.

It's only human nature to put off going to a doctor until you need one. But that doesn't bode well for preventing an illness from occurring—and by then some options for curing the illness may already be off the table. It's the same with your finances. People tend to go to their accountant either to have their taxes prepared or *after* they have a tax problem. I've often wondered this: If paying taxes wasn't required, would accountants *ever* have anyone come in for preventative medicine—that is, to make sure they have a plan in place for their financial security now, in retirement, and, beyond that, for their children?

It is commonplace for people to think, "I know I should look into this, but . . ."—and then they don't. It even crosses the minds of many do-it-yourselfers to see an accountant at some point, if only to make sure they're on the right track. But if you wait till you're sick to see the doctor, it's too late to keep you from getting sick in the first place. The same holds true for visits to your financial advisor.

Reading this book should make you think about visiting your accountant for more than just year-end taxes; you need preventive care and maintenance, too.

Of all the chapters in this book, this has probably been the most challenging one to write because it involves my own profession. As a CPA myself, of course, I have a soft spot for other accountants, especially those in smaller firms like mine. This is the kind of firm that most of you will need, unlike the mega-wealthy with major financial assets, properties, and investments, who gravitate toward big accounting firms. The reason this chapter has been so difficult to write is that what I said about picking a financial advisor in Chapter 3 goes for picking an accountant, too.

A professional designation is important: You should work with an accountant who is licensed, and I recommend a licensed CPA (but I might be prejudiced). Nevertheless, a license is not the whole ballgame. There are accountants without professional designations but with many years of valuable hands-on work experience from which you can benefit. Such people might work with or for a licensed CPA. There are also *enrolled agents* who might not be CPAs but usually are top professionals when it comes to preparing personal and business tax returns. They typically have hands-on experience in dealing with the IRS as well. So don't simply dismiss an accountant out of hand just because he or she isn't a CPA.

Also, a professional designation alone does not mean that the accountant will have the necessary knowledge about the taxation of retirement accounts aspect of retirement distribution planning. As is the case among financial advisors, many accountants know little about this subject. However, accountants are in a worse position because most people assume they do have expertise in this area—that they *must* because it has to do with taxes. That, unfortunately, is not the case. There are complex niche areas in our tax laws that require niche expertise as well. So, while most CPAs in public practice are very knowledgeable, specific situations call for expertise that your CPA may or may not have. You won't know unless you ask.

Accountants, like attorneys (whom I will discuss in Chapter 5), tend to be more generalists than specialists, but they may have specialized knowledge about taxes and tax planning for businesses and industries where they have many clients. For example, when I began my career as an accountant I worked for a firm that did the accounting for one of the biggest carpet companies in the country. The company had stores everywhere in our area, and our firm would do the monthly accounting and financial statements for all these stores. So if you were a carpet or home decorating retailer, our firm was *the* place to go for your accounting needs because we knew your type of business inside and out.

I realized the value of specialization early in my accounting career when, even after attending days of training programs each year and doing hundreds of personal and business tax returns, I constantly seemed to be getting hit with questions in areas in which I just wasn't up to speed. I would try to find the answers and help the client as best I could, and that usually worked out. But eventually I realized I could not learn it all—and that if I did, I would probably wind up in a rubber room, unable to help anybody. So I began to put together a support team, referring certain topics to specialists who worked exclusively in those areas, which is something your accountant should be willing to do, too.

One tax expert whom I really look up to is Robert Katz, senior partner in the law firm of Katz, Bernstein & Katz, LLP, on Long Island, New York. If you ask me, he is the most brilliant tax expert I have ever known. I have been taking his tax and estate planning courses for years. In fact, I took my CPA review courses from him at Hofstra University after completing college. He is renowned as the "tax expert's expert." So imagine my amazement when he called *me* with a tax question about IRAs and trusts! I share this with you not to pat myself on the back (though the call did make my day) but as further evidence that even the savviest of accountants and experts should not be averse to calling on outside expertise when they need it.

1. Know Who You Are and Where You Are

Choosing the right accountant depends to a large extent on what you want the accountant for—individual tax preparation, bookkeeping, auditing, consulting, not-for-profit planning, business tax preparation, financial statements, personal financial planning, estate/retirement planning, payroll services? If the accountant is simply a tax preparer and you're the owner of a small business with a hundred employees and tax issues connected with providing a 401(k) and health care, a straightforward tax preparer won't do.

Even if all you need from the accountant is to review your taxes at the end of the year, you should still look for one capable of doing more than that because your goal should be to start doing at least some minimal financial planning, too. That way your accountant won't be saying to you every tax season, "What'd you do? You should have asked me about that before going ahead with it. *Now we can't fix it!*"

Your accountant should know your marital status. For example, if you are divorced or separated, how should you file? Does he or she have experience with divorced individuals? If you have a divorce issue, you should pick someone who specializes in splitting assets in a divorce settlement, not a generalist who might not know the lay of the land.

Have you lost your job as a result of the recent financial crisis and need advice on the tax options for the lump-sum distribution from your 401(k) plan? One mistake there can wipe out your account in minutes by subjecting it to premature taxation. Does the accountant know about the tax break for appreciated stock in the plan? It's called *net unrealized appreciation* (NUA). If he or she is not aware of that (and many CPAs are not), then maybe you need to work with a CPA who does possess that specialized knowledge, which is so important to you at this time in your life—or see if your accountant would be willing to work with your financial planner, who does have knowledge in this area.

Are you retired or about to retire and will be (or already are) subject to required minimum distributions from your IRA or company plan? Your accountant needs to know this about you, and you need to know whether he or she has expertise in this area of tax planning. It is not just about recording taxable distributions after the fact; it's about doing the planning ahead of time so the taxes can be managed as efficiently and beneficially as possible.

Do you have children who are required to file tax returns? Those returns can be complicated—and costly—especially when your children go to college and have jobs out of state. I remember a client whose child was a real traveler. He had W-2 forms from six different states. What a nightmare those tax returns were. It took three times longer to complete the child's return than his parents' return—and I had to bill them more, too!

If you own a business or intend to, does the accountant have expertise in that type of business and what kind of business entity should you form? Is your accountant open to working with your business or personal attorney and other financial advisors? That's pretty important to know up front.

Will you be doing some record keeping? If not, that's okay, but you still have to be somewhat organized about keeping basic bills and documents. The more you can give your accountant, the more valuable time he or she can spend at tax season doing real tax planning for you instead of organizing your receipts.

These are just some of the items that you need to share with the accountant so that he or she will know who you are and where you are.

2. Educate Yourself

What to Know

When you are considering buying a house, you should have some knowledge of the process going in, or you could wind up in a money pit or worse. The foreclosure debacle going on in the United States as I write these words is proof of that. No, you don't have to be an *expert* on home construction, building codes, mortgage finance, and so on, but you *should* know the basics, if only to avoid being sold a bill of goods.

It's the same with picking an accountant. You should be able to have an intelligent conversation with him or her about money—especially *your* money! The less you know, the more it's going to cost you—because accountants' fees are generally based on time. The less you know when consulting with them, the more time you will take up, and the more money you will spend by having to schedule more consultative visits in order to constantly provide the accountant with more personal information.

The better educated you are about the kind of help you need—be it tax preparation or financial planning—the better you will be able to gauge whether the accountant has the kind of education and expertise to provide that help, and the more productive the consultation will be. Suppose you've read about some tax-saving trick that you think might also work for you, and you bring it up to the accountant. You can feel satisfied when the accountant says, "That's true. But you can do these three other things, too, with better results." And that's what picking the right accountant is really all about.

What to Look For

Anybody can call him- or herself a tax preparer or an accountant. But not everybody can call him- or herself a CPA. That's a professional designation; you have to pass an intensive, comprehensive exam and maintain educational requirements to get and keep it. If the accountant has no professional designation, this doesn't necessarily mean he or she is incompetent and therefore wrong for you. What it does mean, though, is that the accountant is not *answerable* to any legislative, disciplinary, or state regulatory agency or body. Licenses, especially professional licenses like that of CPA, must be maintained to certain standards, or they can and will be revoked. Having a CPA license revoked can put that accountant out of business, leaving you where? So, there's a lot to be said for working with licensed professionals, including accountants.

Stability is another plus. My accounting firm has been in the same location for almost thirty years. That says to my clients, "We're not going anywhere. We're here for you for the long haul." Of course, this doesn't mean a young accountant just starting out won't be there for you for the long haul. Everybody starts out. But in that case, ascertain whether the rookie accountant expresses a genuine interest in your business and in you and is not just paying lip service. You can sense that about people. The more eager novice accountants are about growing their own business, the more undivided attention you will get from them and the more *accessible* they will be when something comes up. That's a concern—you should be able to sleep at night without worrying whether you can get your accountant on the phone or schedule an appointment should the need arise. Furthermore, you need that accessibility year-round, not just at tax time—as is the case with storefront tax preparers, who set up shop for a few months every spring and aren't around for the rest of the year.

Find out what alliances the accountant has and what professional organizations he or she belongs to. As a small-firm practitioner, I knew I had to network with other CPAs and professional advisors to hear other points of view in order to stay abreast of the kind of planning and tax issues they were facing—and that I would face, too, at some point. This is not the kind of learning that can easily be obtained from books. The accountant needs to be *involved* in the profession. For example, early in my career, I would get together with ten or fifteen other CPAs on the first Tuesday night of every month at one of our homes to sit around discussing tax problems we had each encountered in our respective business. This was of immeasurable value to me as a real, in-the-trenches educational experience. We continued those get-togethers for years. Later, joining the New York State Society of CPAs was another of the best moves I ever made. I met colleagues there whose expertise I have relied on for years. I also have been a longtime member of the National Conference of CPA Practitioners, a great organization that supports the needs of smaller CPA firms like mine. Likewise, I joined the Estate Planning Council of New York City, since much of the tax planning I do includes estate planning.

Pound for pound, as far as advisors go, I believe you get the biggest bang for your buck with a great accountant.

Where to Look

Always the best place to start looking for an accountant is a personal referral—provided that referral comes from someone in a situation comparable to yours. For example, what might not work out is a referral from an associate or acquaintance worth millions of dollars in assets, while you're worth, say, $800,000. That person will probably be using a large accounting firm, which may not be the best fit for your needs. So keep to personal referrals from folks who are in the same financial ballpark as you.

Here are some online resources for checking credentials or locating a qualified accountant near you:

- **www.natptax.com** The National Association of Tax Professionals (NATP) is a nonprofit organization that serves the continuing education needs of professionals who work in all areas of tax planning—not just tax preparers, but also attorneys, CPAs, and financial planners. Just click on Find a Tax Professional at the top and you can search by zip code or distance (to a maximum of one hundred miles) for a member tax law specialist near you.

- **www.cpadirectory.com** This is the largest online database of CPAs in the country. Search for names and background information by industries serviced, services provided, or city, state, and zip code.

- **www.acountantsworld.com** This is an extensive database of more than thirty-five thousand CPAs, accountants, and tax pre-parers nationwide, with full details including address, phone numbers, services offered, and specializations. You can search for names by zip code, city, or state.

- **www.naea.org** The National Association of Enrolled Agents is a database of more than eleven thousand independent, licensed tax professionals called *enrolled agents* (EA) across the country. Members are required to complete a minimum of thirty hours of continuing professional education each year in the interpreta-tion, application, and administration of federal and state tax laws in order to maintain membership in the organization. This re-quirement surpasses the IRS required minimum of sixteen hours per year. Search by zip code, city, or state.

3. Avoid Mistakes

Overpaying what they owe in taxes is the biggest mistake people make, and very often they are completely unaware they are doing it. I'm not talking about overpaying on your withholding tax—you'll likely get that overpayment back in a refund check from the IRS. I'm talking about *excessive taxation* as a result of missing out on many bona fide opportunities to reduce your tax liability by hundreds, if not thousands, of dollars—money you could have put to far better use in building a nest egg. That overpayment will not come back to you in a refund check. And there will be no let-ter forthcoming from the IRS expressing its gratitude for adding more to its coffers than you had to. Nor will there be any heads-up from the IRS making sure you're aware of a particular tax break. The responsibility to overpay or pay only what you owe is on *your* shoulders—and those of the accountant you've hand-picked to guide you.

When I was more of a practitioner, I constantly attended full-day seminars to learn about new tax rules and stay on top of the intricacies of the U.S. tax system. All good accountants do that—and that commitment on their part can save you a hundred, or even a thousand, times their fee. So don't make the mistake of basing your hiring decision on the accountant's fee alone. It is the value added that counts.

Always, *always,* avoid the "I know it all" type. One thing I can say about my profession is that accountants take more continuing education courses than any other service professionals I know. They have to learn all they can to stay on top of the always-changing tax laws, loopholes, and new tax-saving strategies and options. Good accountants never claim to know it all.

Some CPAs have begun to play the field by managing the assets of their clients and even selling investments. You should be aware of this in advance—being a good accountant for you does not automatically make that person a good investment advisor for you. The ideal scenario is probably to work with an accountant who is willing to partner with an investment advisor. That way, it's okay if the accountant gets a commission on your investments—you have to pay someone (even if you manage your investments yourself using a fund company, you still pay an asset management fee). So it's to your advantage to get the best of both worlds for the same fee.

Ask your prospective accountant what happens if you receive one of those dreadful letters from the IRS that says "audit." This may happen, and often it can be easily, but not quickly, cleared up. What is the accountant's process for handling audits—and what are the charges? My firm includes this in the fee we charge for preparing your taxes, but if the IRS audit gets too involved or you have to be legally represented at the audit, there would be an extra charge for the additional time, expertise, and expense of preparing for it.

I've made the point before, but it is worth emphasizing the importance of recognizing an accountant's limitations as well as his or her strengths when you make your decision about whose services to use. The accountant might not be an expert in the area where you most need help.

4. Don't Be Shortsighted

Top FAQs . . .

Q: "Ed, I saw a medical show once that said the key to being phys- ically healthy is never to lie to your doctor. Does that go for ac- countants, too—do you have to be as open and honest?"

A: "You do if you want to be financially healthy. It's all about the re- lationship. The more forthright and accurate you are about your circumstances, the better the accountant can help you—not just by saving you a few dollars and cents come April 15, but with big-picture items such as estate and distribution planning, and mining the tax code to wind up with more than you had."

The ideal is to build a relationship with your accountant that will last. The more the accountant gets to know you, the better the service he or she can provide for you—and the better the entire re- lationship will work, as long as you follow through on at least some of the professional advice and counsel you're being given. I have found that my best clients actually do listen to what I say. But there are always some clients to whom I or my staff will suggest strategies and offer recommendations, only to find, when they come back to us, that they haven't done anything.

So don't be shortsighted and assume the relationship is only one way; it's two-way. Accountants' reputations are tied to how sig- nificantly their clients benefit from heeding their tax-saving advice. Mutual success is the means by which the relationship lasts.

5. *Take Action in Small, Consistent Steps*

The first thing you need to do before choosing an accountant is go through the four previous steps. You have to define who you are and exactly what services you need. You need to be as educated about the subject as possible, and you need to make sure your CPA is well educated in that subject, too, and continues that education on a regular basis. Your aim is for a long-term relationship, so don't make a quick decision. That's the point of this last step, which is to take action incrementally so that it ultimately leads to making the right choice. Get some referrals from people you trust and respect and who have financial issues similar to yours, then make an appointment with the first prospect. Make an appointment with another, and then another. The best way to find the person who is right for you is to learn a bit from each one you interview. CPAs will be happy to share their tax philosophies with you. They will be happy to show you course manuals from the various tax courses they have taken. They will also be happy to give you references from satisfied clients, so don't be afraid to ask. If you are married, you and your spouse should interview candidates together so that both of you hear what they have to say and can discuss it later. You will be amazed at how much you will learn from the interview process.

Once you have made your choice, the goal is to establish a long-term relationship. In my experience, relationships with accountants generally last a long time. In fact, they are more enduring than many marriages. I remember getting a call from the daughter of one of my clients. She said she had some tax issues. "What tax issues could *you* possibly have?" I asked, thinking of her, as I always did, as still a kid. She said, "I'm married and I'm an attorney." "But you're only twelve years old!" I answered. That's how long I'd been the accountant for this family. I guess time does pass quickly.

If, however, the fit turns out not to be right, don't hesitate to move on to another CPA who might be better for you. Remember, this is all about you and how comfortable you are working with your accountant.

SAMPLE ACTION STEPS

- Act now—don't wait for an emergency.
- Solicit personal referrals.
- Be prepared—learn more about M-O-N-E-Y.
- Listen.
- Follow through incrementally.

Chapter 5

PICKING THE *RIGHT* ATTORNEY
FOR *YOU*

A son can bear with composure the death of his father, but the loss
of his inheritance might drive him to despair.

—Niccolo Machiavelli

The Gold Mine or the Shaft?

Picking the right divorce lawyer can mean the difference between
getting the gold mine or getting the shaft. This chapter isn't about
choosing a good divorce lawyer but about finding legal expertise in
the complex area of protecting your gold mine from claim jumpers—
and keeping it from becoming played out.

Here, too, a bad pick could cost you and your family big-time.
Your only alternative might then be to just sit back and watch with
a tearful eye as all the money you've spent years building up swirls
down the government drain.

1. Know Who You Are and Where You Are

The process of finding attorneys who are knowledgeable about
asset distribution and inheriting an estate (key plays in the winning
half of the game that I'll explore in Chapters 11 and 13) is very
much a function of this first step.

"Most people who are just starting out don't have enough assets to begin worrying about distribution planning and estate taxes, so they don't require any specialized legal advice yet," says my friend Sy Goldberg, nationally recognized "tax attorney's tax attorney" and veteran expert, who trains attorneys in the arcane tax rules and complex tax strategies of wealth protection and preservation, and is the senior partner in Goldberg & Goldberg, PC, on Long Island, New York. (www.goldbergira.com).

"The average investor usually doesn't start looking for someone like me until he or she hits around fifty—because by then people have been putting money away for a good number of years. Maybe they have a couple of hundred thousand in their retirement fund. It's then that the person says, 'Hey, I've built up a pretty good nest egg here, I better start thinking about making sure to hold onto as much of it as possible.' That's where a good tax and estate planning attorney comes in."

Regardless of age, the minute you begin accumulating valuable assets, you need to look for an attorney to help you protect those assets—not just from taxes, but also from creditors, business associates, and even family members. By "valuable assets" I don't just mean cash and a home, either. I also mean your children and other loved ones; they need you to have a will—perhaps even life insurance and a trust set up, too—in the event you are struck by an illness or die prematurely.

As with selecting any type of advisor, it is important to inventory yourself. What do you own? How is your property owned? Whom do you want to protect? What issues are you worried about? Is your health or that of a loved one such an issue? Will money be needed for nursing home costs now or potentially down the road? Will you need to protect savings from being consumed by health care costs? Once you have identified these issues and potential problem areas, you are well on your way to choosing the right attorney for you because you will be looking for one with expertise in those areas.

A theme has emerged in these chapters on picking advisors,

and that theme applies to picking attorneys as well. There are generalists and there are specialists. If you have specific issues, such as protecting your retirement savings with a trust after you die, then you certainly need not only an estate planning attorney but one with specialized knowledge in the taxation of retirement plan distributions. Again, as with the other professional advisors, I'm sorry to say that even most estate planning attorneys don't have this knowledge, so your search will be more difficult. A good starting place is an advisor or accountant who understands these nuances and can recommend an attorney who likewise understands them.

If your attorney does *not* have specialized knowledge in retirement distribution planning, real estate, divorce, bankruptcy, starting a business, or whatever your individual needs are, be sure that he or she is open to working with your other advisors (financial planner, CPA) who do.

2. Educate Yourself

What to Know

As we learned in the presidential campaign of 2008 when one of the candidates defined being wealthy as having $5 million or so in assets, most of us don't fall into that bracket. We're just scratching by if we have half that. But seriously, it is not uncommon (or wasn't prior to the 2008 economic meltdown) for large numbers of middle-class Americans to retire, after years of saving and investing, with accounts of a million dollars or more. Depending on how many other assets you might have in the form of property and so on, estate tax won't be a problem because the federal estate tax exemption is (as of 2009) up to $3.5 million for singles and $7 million for married couples who plan properly. But if your IRA, coupled with the rest of the assets in your estate, tops these exemptions, you and your tax attorney will have some serious strategizing to do.

Exactly what kind of attorney will you need for this? A tax lawyer? An estate planning attorney? Perry Mason?

"Tax attorneys specialize in the technical and legal side of tax law," says Sy Goldberg. "The type of attorney you will need is one who *can integrate the retirement assets you have into an overall estate plan* should the likelihood exist that you will have a taxable estate at death and your heirs will have to file an estate tax return." You can't just look at the retirement distribution alone as a separate issue, he stipulates. "You have to have someone who knows how to incorporate both the normal assets of an estate [the home, etc.] and the retirement assets [IRAs] into a single, effective, tax-saving, wealth-preserving plan."

If your tax lawyer is unfamiliar with estate planning techniques for eliminating the so-called death tax (a euphemism for a tax on your estate), such as a living trust, a dynasty trust, or a foundation, that's a big problem. Conversely, if your estate planning attorney is unaware of IRS retirement distribution rules, that is also a major issue. And the dual capability is not widespread, Goldberg contends. That's true. In fact, an estate planning attorney once told me off the record that he hopes his clients spend all of their retirement funds before they die so that he does not have to deal with those assets in their estate because the rules are so complicated and he is deathly afraid of making an expensive mistake. He was being honest with me, and I'll bet many other attorneys are privately thinking the same thing.

"A lot of attorneys are taking courses with me now to learn how to dovetail both disciplines, retirement planning and estate planning," Goldberg explains. "So it's important for consumers to learn enough about the two disciplines themselves [see Part III] to be able to ask questions of their attorneys pertinent to discovering whether the attorney can, in fact, handle both."

What to Look For

"I would be very pointed in my questioning," urges Goldberg on the subject of connecting with tax and estate planning attorneys. "Ask if they know the IRA distribution rules. Many have not read them or even taken a course to fathom them. Can they integrate the trust portion of the estate with an IRA trust—in fact do they know what an IRA trust is [see Chapter 13], and how it works? Do they know the trust rules of the state? Can they handle the filing of the trust returns and accounting reports?"

It is also important to determine whether the attorney has an awareness of the Uniform Principal and Income Act (UPAIA). The stated purpose of this act is to provide homogeneous procedures to govern the proper distribution of assets to trust beneficiaries and heirs by trustees and estate plan administrators. It is applicable across forty of the fifty states and has changed a lot of the definitions that apply to an IRA trust.

"I've found that there are not a lot of training programs available in these states on the trust accounting rules, so you really have to put the attorney to the test to see what he or she knows," says Goldberg. "Tax lawyers are generally not involved in trust administration. So as you are setting up a trust, or if you are the trustee, you will want to know what plans the attorney has considered and recommends for administering the trust now and for the next forty, fifty, or sixty years after you and the attorney are gone. These are not issues or concerns with cookie-cutter solutions."

Creditor protection is another big issue you should not overlook or neglect to bring up. Forty-one states currently take the position that the beneficiary of an inherited retirement account is *not* protected from creditor claims against the individual from whom the account was inherited. In other words, if you go through some tough financial times in your life and die still owing money, all but nine states say that the accumulated assets in the retirement account you bequeath to, say, your children are fair game for your unpaid creditors after you've departed the scene. And even if *you* live in one of those nine states but your named IRA beneficiaries do not, and you want to be sure their inheritance is secure from your creditors, you and they have a problem—because the courts will look to the jurisdiction where the *beneficiaries reside*. This is all the more reason to have an attorney with experience in the effective use of trusts as a wealth preservation tool; irrevocable trusts are typically the primary solution to this situation.

Where to Look

Most people think of tax or estate attorneys as the cavalry that comes to the rescue when the IRS is breathing down their necks. And it is true that they specialize in helping taxpayers solve tax issues with the government. But perhaps even more important, they have to be able to provide and execute a strategy for their clients' investment and estate needs that avoids tax problems in the first place.

As with choosing a financial advisor or accountant, the way to start the attorney selection process is through word of mouth. Whom do your friends and business acquaintances use and recommend? Have these attorneys, in fact, executed and administered an estate plan for them or anyone else? Any licensed attorney can draw up a document. Executing an estate or IRA distribution tax plan is a horse of a different color. Contact your local bar association for the background information and credentials of anyone who is referred to you; this is also a good source for locating additional prospects.

If you must expand your search for a tax or estate attorney, here are some key online resources you can use.

- **www.abanet.org** The American Bar Association (ABA) is the largest voluntary professional association in the world. With more than four hundred thousand members, the ABA provides continuing legal education information about the law, including estate planning, wills, probate, and trust programs, to assist lawyers in their work for clients and in initiatives to improve the legal system for the public. A special Section of Taxation provides the most current information and analysis for tax lawyers and tax professionals. To locate ABA members in your area, go to the ABA's alternate site, www.findlegalhelp.org, and search by state.

- **www.SaveWealth.com** According to the website, this online network screens qualified estate attorneys across the country for inclusion in its member directory. The site then provides detailed profiles and biographical data for each member to help consumers make informed decisions. Some of the legal practitioners listed in the directory have also provided the site with articles, testimonials, or a profile link. In addition, the site provides a subdirectory of living-trust attorneys throughout the United States who have their own sites.

• **www.irahelp.com** Ed Slott's IRA Advisor Group also includes some attorneys who have had the benefit of access to the same extensive training in IRA distribution and estate planning as all of our other financial services members. You can find them at my website. If you cannot find an attorney in your area, contact one of our Elite advisor members in your location. Since they know how important it is for their own clients to have the right attorney, they may be able to offer you a referral that is worth checking out.

3. Avoid Mistakes

When casting a wide net to find a tax and estate planning attorney, be sure to focus on attorneys who are licensed to practice in *your* state. This is critical, especially in the field of estate planning—and most particularly in trust planning—as tax codes differ from state to state and are constantly changing.

Unless they are like Sy Goldberg, a former professor of tax law who trains tax attorneys in many states on changing trust and other estate planning tax rules and regulations, most tax attorneys have a tough time keeping up with these changes in their own states, let alone in other states. "It's very difficult for them to be able to devote themselves to the hundreds of hours I can to interpreting the account and trust application rules of so many states," says Goldberg. "So stay local if you can." Go for someone who has training and experience in your state's rules rather than someone who is licensed to practice in more than one state.

I would even go as far as asking if the candidate has heard of either Sy Goldberg or Natalie Choate, an IRA and estate planning expert and author of the indispensable *Life and Death Planning for Retirement Benefits*. If your candidate has not heard of them, and if you have a retirement account to protect and need a trust, don't employ this attorney. Sy and Natalie are the gold standard for attorneys in this area. If your attorney has never heard of either of them, it is a good bet that he or she has never opened a book, magazine, or professional journal on the topic.

4. Don't Be Shortsighted

As mentioned, most investors don't go to a tax and estate planning attorney until they have accumulated some assets to protect and preserve—typically, a minimum of around $100,000 to start. Thus, most attorneys anticipate that the average investor will not start planning until then. Nevertheless, it's never too early to begin learning the language of IRA distribution and estate preservation and acquiring an understanding of the tools involved so that you are ready to talk knowledgeably with the tax attorney you hire when the day finally comes. As a practical matter, this knowledge will really help you to select an experienced, multidisciplined attorney who can help keep you and your heirs from being fleeced.

Always remember to focus on the long-term big picture. This means that even if you don't have much when you start out, you should nevertheless lay the groundwork for at least protecting those funds for you and your loved ones later on. And if you have accumulated a sizable retirement account and want to leave a tax-efficient legacy to the next generation through a trust, then you need to find a qualified attorney now.

5. Take Action in Small, Consistent Steps

To sum everything up, our tax laws, particularly in the areas of IRA distribution and estate planning, are complicated and always changing. In my state of New York, for example, major changes in the trust laws were enacted by the legislature in 2008, after having already undergone a host of other major changes as recently as 2002! So, unless you are a specialist yourself, it is guaranteed that you will need a tax and estate planning attorney at some stage of your investing and wealth-building life to stay on top of things for yourself and your family.

This process can take a while. It is important to take a few steps now to stay on track. Here's how to go about it: First, determine whether you need an attorney; then start your search with referrals. Get your financial advisor, your accountant, and your family involved in the process, too—especially the latter, since your family will be the beneficiaries of your decision making and it is in their best interests to make sure those decisions play out properly.

SAMPLE ACTION STEPS

- Be direct in your questions.
- Bring up creditor protection.
- Stay local.
- Get your family involved.
- Learn the basic language of IRA distribution planning and estate planning.

Part II

THE FIRST HALF OF
THE GAME

"I have no idea what the stock market is going to do next month or six months from now. I do know that the American economy, over a period of time, will do very well, and people who own a piece of it will do well."

—Warren Buffett

Chapter 6

BECOME AN INSTANT SAVER

I've got all the money I'll ever need if I die by four o'clock.
—Henny Youngman, comedian

More, More, More

If there's one message from Part I that I hope calls out to you loud and clear by now, it's this: Accumulating wealth and keeping it require a plan—for saving, investing smartly, and, in the end, keeping your accumulation from being diminished by taxes.

If you don't create such a plan, you will get the government's plan. That's how the government gets all its money—from taxpayers who don't plan.

In this first chapter of Part II, we're going to get down to the brass tacks of laying out your plan. It's pretty straightforward. I call this plan for staying rich for life "More, More, More":

- *More money for you now*

- *More money for your retirement*

- *More money for your loved ones*

And more of it tax free—in some cases, all of it tax free!

The First "More"

The first "More" starts with saving *now* (if you aren't saving already) so that your savings *can* continue to grow through the magic of compounding. Investing smartly—knowing where to put some of the money you're saving so that it *will* grow, as safely as possible— is the part of the process addressed in Chapter 7 ("Investment Strategies for Now and Later"); it is the second leg of the journey to achieving the first "More." This journey is equivalent to the *first half* of the game, using our football analogy.

Savings accounts and investment portfolios can withstand many more financial blows during the phase in which you are working toward the first "More"—in other words, the *accumulation phase*. This is because you have a lot of time to recoup any losses and rebuild your wealth. If you find yourself in a bad market scenario once you get to the second half of the game—the distribution phase, in which you start to draw dollars off your savings to live on during retirement—then your wealth can implode, killing your chances of achieving the second "More." Thus, during the first half of the game, you can weather more storms, regardless of your age, than you can in the distribution phase because your focus in the accumulation phase is on *saving consistently*.

Of course, the operative word in the previous paragraph is *saving*. As we all know from both the mainstream and the financial news, the United States ranks fairly low among the world's nations that save. I don't mean to sound like an old fogy, but it is typically younger Americans who keep this ranking low—and for a very simple reason. Almost as a rule, younger Americans *don't save because they aren't taught, and thus they haven't learned how.*

It's almost part of the culture in the United States that very few young people entering the workforce are concerned about tomorrow. They're focused on *today*—on acquiring that new car or a new iPod— they seek instant gratification. They're unconcerned about how money works and how saving money can make it grow. Therefore, few acquire the ethic of saving (at least, perhaps, not until they're much older) or the discipline required to put that ethic to work.

Conversely, older generations of Americans tend to be better savers, but even among these groups many incline toward using their savings (and other assets such as their homes) like ATM machines whenever they need cash. Doing this actually sabotages their hard work by cashing out some of their savings.

So let's apply the five steps to starting on the path toward achieving the first "More." Here you will pick up some general information, tips, and techniques to help you become an instant and lifelong disciplined saver—without having to scrimp (well, not too much) or overtax your brainpower.

1. Know Who You Are and Where You Are

It's never too late to start saving. Even if you are older when you begin to save, it's better late than never to create your own plan rather than going with the government plan, which is to accumulate wealth for *Uncle Sam.*

It's true: You have to *force yourself* to save money. And you have to keep forcing yourself until that discipline becomes ingrained. You also have to have a long-range goal to help see you through the times when you'll be feeling a little frustrated at the process and question why you're doing all this. Therefore, it goes without saying that those who start saving earlier in their lives will automatically have a lot more leeway and choices open to them than someone who starts to save at, say, age forty-five.

FYI . . .

Life changes and throws you curves, financial and otherwise. The sooner you begin to save—however small the amount may be at first—the more flexibility you will have to safely sidestep those curves. Someone starting later in life has less room to maneuver. It's as simple as that.

Time to catch up is a pervasive concern today among many savers, especially those close to retirement, whose accounts have been hit hard by the tanking stock market. Although you may be behind the eight ball through no fault of your own, the fact that you have been a lifelong saver and have built up some wealth—even if it is somewhat depleted now—means you are not as far behind as many others. You can still catch up by rebalancing your portfolio between safer income-producing investments and riskier growth products. Also, there's a special provision in the tax code that says if you are at least age fifty by the end of the tax year, you can sock away an additional $1,000 in your IRA or Roth IRA, or an additional $5,500 (in 2009) in your 401(k), 403(b), or 457 plan or Roth 401(k) or Roth 403(b), to help you catch up. In fact, it's called the *catch-up provision*. For future years, the additional catch-up amount increases with inflation.

There is another provision in the tax code designed to encourage the saving habit among people of any age who find it difficult to do so because they earn low incomes. It's called a *saver's credit*. If your income is below a certain level, the IRS gives you a nonrefundable tax credit of up to $1,000 for contributions that you make to your 401(k) or IRA—and in addition to that, you get a tax deduction for the contribution. Depending on how much (or, more likely, how little) you make and the deductions that you're eligible for, you probably won't even have to pay for your contribution, which adds up to funding your retirement account for free! This is something to look into if you have suffered a job loss and your income falls, which might make you eligible for the credit. Every dollar counts in this case, so don't overlook this possibility.

Of course, neither I nor any financial advisor would recommend making savings, investment, or retirement plan contributions at all costs. You have to look at your financial profile. It makes little sense to fund any of those items if you have to pull out a credit card when you go to the supermarket. But the saver's credit is a way to get you on the road to saving money, or to keep you on that road, whether you are just starting out or at any stage of your life in which you are low on money but still paying taxes. Even though investing, saving for a home or a college education, or funding a retirement account is the last thing on your mind at such a time because you're concerned about putting food on the table, you can still become an instant saver.

There is no magic bullet. Your expenses, including taxes, are lower at your current age than they will ever be again. So you had better start tightening your belt. *You have to.*

2. Educate Yourself

Back in the bad old days when I was going to high school, we were offered some courses in business and "life skills," in which we learned about such things as how to open a savings account, the meaning of *compound interest* and how it worked, and how to balance a checkbook. This is not the norm in high schools anymore. As a result, young people can graduate from high school today with little or no concept of money except how to spend it——they may not even know how to write a check.

The opening chapters of this book offer numerous suggestions for educating yourself about money and where to look for the most unbiased information. Here is an additional resource aimed at beginning savers of any age, but at younger folks in particular: Go talk to Grandma or Grandpa if they're still living, or an elderly friend or acquaintance, because they might remember an earlier period of economic turbulence, such as the Great Depression of the 1930s or World War II. They would therefore be aware of what it is like to have to conserve resources and save for a rainy day; they couldn't just walk into a showroom on a whim and buy themselves that hot new GPS for their car or a FlipHD camcorder.

Ask them, "What was it like when you were my age and what did *you* do?" They'll be able to tell you plenty of ways to save a nickel here and there and develop a savings habit, such as putting off major purchases until they could afford them and opening a Christmas Club account at the bank to accumulate cash for the holidays so they wouldn't have to go into debt to buy gifts.

This is an excellent source of *practical* guidance about how to become an instant saver. Then you can add to your knowledge by reading all the interviews you can find at your local library or on the Internet with well-known high-net-worth investors such as Warren Buffett—older-generation money experts who grew up stone poor and became rich by always "paying themselves first" rather than spending every dime as soon as it came into their hands.

Even just a small measure of knowledge gained from this thrifty generation should be enough to at least get you started in the direction of becoming a supersaver.

3. Avoid Mistakes

Some people play tricks on themselves in order to save. Tricks don't work. It is mind-set and discipline that count. For example, you might open a 401(k) and put money into it solely because this theoretically makes it harder for you to get at if the impulse to spend strikes, as this impulse most surely will. Then one day you find yourself running a little low on available cash and decide to dip ("just this once") into your 401(k) before you turn 59½, the age at which you are eligible to start withdrawals. When you do this, you have to pay a 10 percent penalty on top of income tax for taking the money out prematurely. Your "putting it out-of-reach" trick has only wound up costing you—and it will keep costing you more and more every time you go back to that well, which you more than likely will, because in the land of temptation there is no such place as "just this once."

Your approach should be that you are putting these dollars away in order to *grow* them, not to create an only slightly out-of-reach piggy bank. Your mind-set must be this: *These dollars are not accessible anymore!* Until you adopt that mind-set, you might be better off putting those dollars in an actual piggy bank on your dresser or under your mattress, where you will incur no penalties on top of taxes for "just this once" withdrawals.

As noted in step 1, understanding yourself and your goals will help you develop the mind-set that saved dollars are no longer accessible dollars; the recognition of why you are saving will always pull you back. Acquiring this mind-set gives you the discipline to look temptation in the eye and say no.

Becoming overwhelmed with debt, particularly credit card debt, is the biggest mistake most people make that prevents them from saving. If you are in this situation, you need to pay off the debt credit card by credit card. So let's say you have five credit cards, and for each credit card you're going to be paying $20 interest per month. Choose the card with the lowest balance and pay that off first. Once you've paid off the first card, the extra $20 can be allocated toward the second credit card, so you pay off the second credit card much more quickly. Once you've paid off the second-lowest balance and credit card, add the extra $40 (from cards one and two) to the payment for the third card and now lowest balance. Keep going until you are out of debt—of course, this also requires you to avoid using your credit cards and creating more debt. Sometimes you have to make a decision: Should I pay off my credit card or should I add to my 401(k) account? If you choose to save in your 401(k) account, where you might be earning 4 percent, and keep that high-interest credit card on which you're paying 18 to 21 percent, the net figure is going to put you in the red. This is definitely going to affect your ability to save over time.

A lot of services are available to help you if you become overextended, but you must be careful because some of these companies are in it just for the money. And if they're going to charge you an arm and a leg just to lower the interest rates on your credit cards or reduce the amount that you owe, you may be able to do that yourself. Call the different credit card companies on your own and say something like this: "I only have $20,000, so I simply can't afford to pay off the balance on the card. But if you give me a lower interest rate and reduce some of the debt it would be more manageable for me." One expert financial advisor suggested this to a client, who was surprised to find that some credit card companies were very willing to cooperate with her plan rather than dig in their heels and risk losing everything. Sometimes you can do for yourself for free what a debt-reducing service promises to accomplish for a hefty fee.

4. Don't Be Shortsighted

Here are some common excuses people make about why they can't save:

- "I don't have enough money!"

- "What's the point of putting aside twenty bucks—where will that get me?"

- "I can't afford to save, no matter what."

Does this sound like you? Then unless you live on Planet X, where there is no Y.O.Y.O. economy, I recommend you change your tune and start thinking like this:

- "I've got to find the money anyway!"

- "A little is better than nothing—especially with compounding."

- "I can't afford *not* to save, no matter what."

The shortsighted view of saving is that it's like dieting—it's all about denying yourself something you want today for the promise of tomorrow. But pushing aside that big slice of double-frosted chocolate cake at lunchtime, say, or not picking up that new pair of Gucci loafers you have a yen for that just went on sale is *not* denying yourself as much as it is deciding to pass on something you know deep down you can live without, something you don't really need *now*. You are just surrendering to the habit of instant gratification. And a habit can be broken—perhaps not easily and not without some effort—but it *can* be broken, if you take the long view.

Here are some strategies for getting past shortsightedness and the mind-set that says, "There's just no way I can squeeze out an extra penny and start saving now."

Keep a record of your *out-of-pocket expenditures* over the course of a week or a month. Write them down in a notebook, or if you're computer oriented and want a more sophisticated tool, use a personal finance software program such as Quicken, Microsoft Money, or Moneydance. At the end of the week or month, check your figures. Financial advisors confirm that the results of this exercise are usually mind-boggling to their clients. "Are you kidding me? What the heck am I doing squandering that much?" clients exclaim. It does amount to squandering money—spending frivolously because it's become a habit.

"Even I have to catch myself from time to time," says one financial advisor. "I have a daily routine. In the morning I get in the car and stop off at Dunkin' Donuts for a coffee and a muffin on the way to work. That's just my morning routine. Then I go out to lunch every afternoon. That's my afternoon routine. And a couple nights a week I go out for something to eat with my wife, or I get together with a friend for a beer, or this or that—my evening routine. Add up all these routines and what I'm spending can run into the hundreds of dollars every month, spending that isn't at all necessary when you come right down to it.

"I can eliminate *all* those 'extras' with a snap of the fingers, of course. But, hey, all work and no play makes Jack a dull boy, right? So, let's say I eliminate 60 percent of them. It's not that difficult to brew a cup of coffee at home three days a week to take to work with me. It's not that demanding to pack a lunch a couple days a week. That's not penny-pinching or scrimping. It's simply being cognizant of where your money is going so you can apply the brakes to at least some of your outlay and put that money to better, longer-term use [by] saving it." Instead of laying out five bucks a day at Starbucks 250 days a year, you could wind up with $1,250 in savings that you can use to open a 401(k) or add to the IRA you've already got.

"Who couldn't eliminate that small amount from their expense budget every year?" this advisor continues. "I'm talking a little over $3 a day! And it's not that hard. Luckily, as humans, we have short memories, so once you change your spending habits, over time you'll forget why you ever felt you 'needed' to indulge it in the first place. You can still enjoy yourself, but you're also saving 10 or 20 percent of your cash every month."

"I put myself on a budget—so I put my kids on a budget," adds this advisor. "They receive a small allowance every week, but I get to hold onto it. When they want something, I'm there to act as a friendly reminder. Each time, I ask: 'Are you sure this is something you *really* want to spend your allowance money on?' And it didn't take long for the frivolousness to slow down quite a bit. As they see their allowance piling up from being more thoughtful [about] how they spend it, they're slowly grasping the concept that *having money* can be cool, too."

I go to my local 7-Eleven many mornings, and almost all the time I see the same people buying the same two expensive items: lottery tickets and cigarettes. And I always think, "Where's the long-term payoff in doing that?" Plus, whenever a state government needs money (which is all the time these days) the first thing it does is raise cigarette taxes, making cigarettes an even bigger expense for these people. Eliminating the cigarettes alone could add up to thousands of dollars over a year for them, and they'd be in better health to enjoy the savings. As far as buying lottery tickets is concerned, I suppose they could make a case for doing that, assuming they've been struck by lightning more than once, the statistical chance of which is about equal to that of winning the lottery. All the state lotteries really are is an extra tax on people who are bad at math. The fact is, you win automatically by *not* playing.

To become a saver, you've got to change your perception of what is and is not a *necessity*. Forced saving is the only way to change that perception. Budgeting is the way to develop the discipline to force saving—and watching your savings grow will, in turn, reinforce the discipline.

Get a pen and some paper and write down every expense you have and every penny you spend each month. Don't try to keep track in your head; that doesn't work. It doesn't matter how small

FYI ...

Say you set aside $1,250 in a 401(k) plan. Let's see how much that figure would grow over a ten-year period at a modest 8 percent rate of return—assuming you don't put in a single extra penny, and you don't touch what's there:

2009:	$1,250.00	plus 8 percent	($100.00)	=	$1,350.00
2010:	$1,350.00	plus 8 percent	($108.00)	=	$1,458.00
2011:	$1,458.00	plus 8 percent	($116.64)	=	$1,574.64
2012:	$1,574.64	plus 8 percent	($125.97)	=	$1,700.61
2013:	$1,700.61	plus 8 percent	($136.04)	=	$1,836.65
2014:	$1,836.65	plus 8 percent	($146.93)	=	$1,983.58
2015:	$1,983.58	plus 8 percent	($158.69)	=	$2,142.27
2016:	$2,142.27	plus 8 percent	($171.38)	=	$2,313.65
2017:	$2,313.65	plus 8 percent	($185.09)	=	$2,498.74
2018:	$2,498.74	plus 8 percent	($199.90)	=	$2,698.64

You've more than doubled your savings! Now imagine what the figure would be if, over the same period, instead of going back to spending frivolously you continued to put an additional $1,250 into that account each year: $19,556.85. Wow! Keep doing the math. The more you save, the more it grows, and the more you have. That's the magic of compounding. In Chapter 7, I will show how to make that magic even stronger with sound investment strategies.

the expenditure might be, write it down—including any contributions you make to your 401(k) or other retirement plan; treat them as part of your budget, so they become a recurring expense every two weeks or every month, or however often you get paid. When you add everything up, if you see that the total exceeds your net income, try to cut back where you can. This should be obvious: If your spending exceeds your income, you will never be able to build real long-term wealth. If saving exceeds spending, even by a small amount, that's enough to get yourself on the right track.

Unfortunately, because of expenses, you might sometimes have to cut back on what you are saving for retirement. For people who envision themselves in this fix, experts recommend that if your employer offers a matching contribution for the company's 401(k) plan, you should try to put in as much as you can early on to get 100 percent of the employer match. It's free money—and that way the total contribution doesn't have to come from you.

Another way to supercharge your saving habit comes from another advisor friend of mine. "I have a lot of friends who are very talented, and they make money from things they enjoy doing outside their regular nine-to-five job," she says. "For instance, one of them likes to bake on the side, and this Christmas she made more than $50,000 selling her cakes. Because of the tough economic times, she didn't want to spend it, which is what she usually would have done, so I recommended that she set up a simplified employee pension individual retirement account [SEP IRA] for the corporation she set up, and put some of that money in it. And from that $50,000, she was able to put away $12,500 on a pretax basis—just from doing what she loves to do.

"So I tell people, always take a step back and look at everything you're doing. If, say, you do some consulting on the side, use some of those extra earnings to get yourself in the habit of saving. The contribution limit for a SEP IRA and other qualified plans is $49,000 in 2009 and increases in future years based on inflation; that's how much you can put away for any sideline work you do. And the fact that you are working for yourself means you can also put away an additional $49,000. So, assuming you made a ton of money on the side and in your regular job, you could be putting away up to $98,000 on a pretax basis in your two retirement accounts ($49,000 from your job plus $49,000 from your sideline business)."

FYI . . .

Save even more by putting your spouse and kids on the payroll. You get a tax write-off for what you pay them for the work they do *that allows you to fund a retirement savings account for each of them and for you!* Just make sure their employment is legitimate and can be substantiated if the IRS comes knocking at your door. It wouldn't be credible to say that your son is helping you with your consulting business if he's only five years old. Stay on the up-and-up.

5. Take Action in Small, Consistent Steps

"I started saving when I was in fourth grade," a client told his financial advisor during their initial consultation. "In fourth grade, everybody in class was given the opportunity to open a passbook savings account in what was then the Home Savings Bank [of Albany, New York]. My folks, both Depression-era babies, encouraged me and I think I started with fifty cents. I always saved after that—even in college when I, along with everybody else, was broke!"

That small step is how you become a saver. Once you get into the habit of saving, you seldom lose it, and you're on your way to staying rich for life.

You've got to start somewhere. If you can stick to a budget for a reasonable period of time, you have a high probability of continuing the instant saving habit over a long period of time.

The key to successful budgeting, like everything else in this book, is to shoot for small but gradual victories. Don't try to cut out everything right away to find money you can save, or your plan will fail. Again, it's like dieting. Cut out all the foods you enjoy for a three-week period, and, guaranteed, at the end of that time you'll wind up eating the refrigerator. When you are trying to develop the instant saving habit, don't begin by biting off more than you can chew.

SAMPLE ACTION STEPS

- Start a forced savings plan—a 401(k), IRA, or even just a passbook savings account to get your feet wet.
- Add to, never subtract from, your savings account accumulations.
- Get saving tips from older, veteran savers.
- Keep a daily, weekly, or monthly record of your expenses to free up cash for saving.
- Budget to build the forced saving discipline and make it a habit.
- Rely on your savings goals to keep overspending on whims in check.

Chapter 7

INVESTMENT STRATEGIES
FOR NOW AND LATER

If a man empties his purse into his head, no man can take it away from him. An investment in knowledge always pays the best interest.
—Benjamin Franklin

Join the Party? Not Always!

Nobody gets rich overnight, except lottery winners—and we all know how few lottery winners there are. Investors who play the financial markets as if they were the lottery usually wind up going broke from taking too many risks. You've heard the philosophy: The greater the risk, the greater the reward. Well, it works the other way, too: The greater the risk, the greater the penalty—if things go badly, you can wind up losing your head *and* your savings.

"My two main rules of investing go like this," says a seasoned financial advisor. "First of all, there is not *always* going to be a party. In other words, sometimes plain old cash is your best investment. There are times to be in the market and there are times not to be in the market. That is what people need to learn because most of them think, 'I *always* need to be invested in the market. I need to sell this or buy that.' That is what Wall Street tells you. Sell this stock because it's not doing well. Or, fly over here and buy this stock and see if you can make up what you just lost. But there are times when you are just better off *not being anywhere*. Now [2008] is one of them. Who wants to be going up 900 points one day and down 500 the next day? It doesn't make any sense to be doing that. Sure it's good to have your toe in the market. But for the most part, if you have 100 percent of your assets in the market right now, you are probably not sleeping too well and neither is your financial advisor—assuming he or she still is your financial advisor! So sometimes cash really is king and it's okay not to play. It really is. You play the game when there is a game to be played, and you don't when there isn't. That's rule number one," says this expert.

"Rule number two is you buy what makes sense out there," this advisor continues. "In other words, if it makes sense to buy income-producing investments, buy income. If it doesn't, then don't. Don't go out and buy income just because you *think* you need income. If it makes sense to be in the stock market and buying growth investments or buying international funds or whatever, then that is what you should be buying. Yes, you should balance yourself a little bit. Don't get me wrong—I don't think my eighty-eight-year-old father should be going out and buying an all-growth international portfolio if that is the hot thing. But if income is really, really low, it doesn't make a lot of sense to force the situation and invest in more of that, either."

1. Know Who You Are and Where You Are

In the world of investing, who you are is your *investor personality,* which is defined as your degree of *risk tolerance.*

Your degree of risk tolerance can be *very different* from your neighbor's down the street. It's like going on a roller coaster. People coming off a ride usually have two widely varying responses. There are those who say, "What a rush, let's do it again!" and others who say, "Where's the restroom? I'm going to be sick!"

It's the same with investing. Some people have a lot more Las Vegas in their blood than others. There are those who are fairly conservative when it comes to investing money but who are also willing to take a calculated risk now and then. And then there are those who are totally averse to taking any kind of risk, long or short term, calculated or not.

Many advisors and brokers contend that determining the genetic makeup of their clients from a financial perspective (i.e., their risk tolerance) is quite often a shot in the dark. Age is seldom the determining factor. For example, a twenty-five-year-old who is just starting to put money into the market and has many years ahead to recoup any short-term losses may reveal him- or herself to be a more conservative investor than someone who is, say, fifty-five years old and looking at retirement ten years down the road.

"It's personality more than age that drives risk tolerance," says an expert financial advisor colleague. "Some people are just innately more aggressive when it comes to money, and that trait was there from the beginning—it probably comes down to how they were taught about money by their parents (if at all) and how they approached risk of any kind even as children. As a result, there are a lot of people today who made a tremendous amount of money because of their more aggressive approach—but the irony is now they don't have two nickels to rub together."

How conservative or aggressive investors are might be in the genes, but the degree may not be evident even to the investors themselves, this expert maintains. "Investors—particularly individual investors, not so much institutional investors like banks—only really learn about themselves during bear markets. Even non-risk-takers tend to become too aggressive during the good times. That's just human nature. It's just greed kicking in. Sometimes it's not even greed as much as 'if it ain't broke, don't fix it.' When things are good and every monthly statement shows your investments increasing in value, why make a change? That's just natural. But during times like the global financial meltdown of 2008, everybody starts questioning every investment they've ever made, and they just want to hide. So it's very difficult for people to articulate to their advisors or brokers how conservative or aggressive they really are—until they open their October statements and see their investments going down 45 or 50 percent on paper in ten months. That's when they're going to learn a lot about who they truly are when it comes to personal finance. Even veteran investors who understand the markets and have experienced ups and downs before may turn conservative in a panic."

As a general rule, most individuals tend to invest more conservatively than they think they are; they tend to invest more aggressively than they probably should—or than they probably can afford to; and they don't know which until gut-check time, says our expert. "But there are ways to better manage your impulses as you bring them into clearer focus," this expert contends. "You do this by *adjusting your approach to investing in the market based on what it is you want to accomplish.* 'Well, I want to be a millionaire at sixty-five,' you say. That's fine. That's a starting point. It says to your advisor and to you that your emphasis should probably be *growth investing,* an approach that comes with higher degrees of risk because it's all about building wealth. And you should probably not be *investing for income* at this stage. You have to make sure that you invest differently during the accumulation years than you do later during your retirement. Your investment philosophy has to change, and your focus later needs to be more along the lines of preservation and distribution as opposed to accumulation, which is intrinsically more risky. But if you are closer in years to that age sixty-five target date, and your goal is to have enough money to cover any heavy-duty medical expenses or nursing home costs in retirement, then

FYI . . .

ASSET ALLOCATION: This is the process of balancing risk and reward over your time horizon by mixing investments among many different asset classes—that is, a percentage of stocks, bonds, cash, and real estate—in your portfolio, in keeping with your long-range goals.

ASSET CLASS: This encompasses different investment categories—stocks, bonds, cash and cash equivalents, real estate, and derivative investments (i.e., options and futures) and precious metals.

BONDS: These are long-term debt securities issued to investors by corporations and national and state governments to help finance current operations or to pay for government programs without increasing taxes.

DERIVATIVES: These are financial instruments whose value derives from the performance of an underlying asset, such as a stock, bond debt, or a commodity like oil. Examples of derivatives are futures contracts, options, and forward contracts. The economic meltdown of 2008, some have said, derived in large part from an overzealous market for derivatives.

GROWTH INVESTMENTS: These consist of stocks and stock funds; dividend payments are minimal if they exist at all, but the annual rate of return is typically well above average. Growth investments are for more aggressive folks with a higher risk tolerance than more conservative types. Due to the volatility of the stock market, growth investments can provide substantial gains, but there is also the risk of substantial losses in the event of a bear market.

INCOME INVESTMENTS: These include stocks offering solid dividends, mutual funds, bank CDs, and other interest-bearing bank accounts, as well as bonds and other debt instruments such as U.S. Treasury bills, plus property such as real estate that is rented out for income.

SECTOR: This is the stock market's grouping of businesses that buy or sell similar goods and services and are, therefore, in direct competition with each other.

STOCKS: These are ownership shares in the equity of a publicly held company or corporation.

you should probably focus your investment choices more on income rather than growth."

It's extremely important to know what you want to achieve so that you can determine what you should be investing in to get there. If you are just out there investing for no real purpose ("Hey, this looks good; I'll buy this today"), you could wind up with a portfolio that's hazardous to your financial health if things go bad, triggering an investing panic attack.

"You have to shop with purpose," another top advisor adds. "It's like going to the grocery store. If you go without a list, you'll probably do a lot of impulse buying and load your cart up with stuff you don't need and [that] is probably bad for you. The best thing my nutritionist did for me was to show me how to put together a shopping list directed at my eating healthier so I'll live longer. If the item isn't on that list it doesn't go in my shopping cart." That is a long-range health strategy with a clear result in mind. Your approach to investing should be the same. You need a long-range strategy with a result in mind to help you determine what goes into your shopping cart. Your list will change just as it will when you go to the grocery store for something and the store doesn't have it—you may need to make a substitution. Having a result in mind ensures the substitution you make is still appropriate to the long-range strategy you've put in place to accomplish the result you seek. "In financial terms, that means knowing whether to put more growth stocks into your asset allocation mix, or more income-earning investments, or a combination of growth and income products—and at what stage to make the adjustment."

2. Educate Yourself

If you are going to invest in the stock market and want to understand what, say, the international fund market is doing, your best source of information and education is the professional you pick to manage your investment portfolio—that is, your financial advisor (see Chapter 3). That's why you need to find the person who is right for you. Advisors get the best, most reliable data in a more concise, easier-to-understand form than we, the public, can get from Internet bloggers or similar sources purporting to be in the know. So don't be afraid or feel intimidated by your lack of knowledge about something to pick up the phone and call your financial advisor to get the information you need about the markets, how they work, and what you can and cannot achieve in them. A good advisor or portfolio manager's stock in trade is knowledge and expertise, so who better to consult to educate yourself about investment strategies?

One colleague of mine tells the following story about how he approaches the education issue. "I met a woman the other day who was in her late thirties or early forties—the accumulation phase of her life. When I told her what I did for a living, she said, 'Oh, I'd be too afraid to put money in the stock market *ever*! That would make me feel really uncomfortable.' And yet she was also worried about not having enough money to live on when she got old, and she wanted to build up a nest egg. So I said to her, 'I'm going to put you on my mailing list, and starting this afternoon, you're going to get some material I've put together for people just like you. I want you to read it; then, over the next couple of weeks, you and I will get together several times for a few hours, and I want you to ask me questions about what you still don't understand about investing or still feel uneasy about. I won't just give you answers but *explanations*— I'm going to *educate you* so that you fully understand the investing process, because it is only through understanding it that you will come to feel comfortable with that process. I send my clients all kinds of stuff—by e-mail so they can access it with the push of a button. I send them material I write, that others write, material that agrees with my approach toward investing, and stuff that doesn't agree. I want them to have as full a picture as possible of what is going on out there."

Investors need to know why they're putting money into a particular product—be it stock, bond, or mutual fund—and what they expect that investment to do for them. This advisor adds, "If I were to call a client and say, 'You own shares in Johnson & Johnson, why?' the client would be able to tell me, because in the planning process I teach my clients why. They will have a pretty good idea of what we're looking for from that investment. For example: Johnson & Johnson is a health care company—Band-Aids, saline, things like that. So it's got low risk—basically because the health care industry is likely to be growing in strength over the next ten years as the baby boom generation gets older. In this way, clients are educated as to why they're in that particular stock, know what they are look-ing for from that stock to achieve their goals, and they grasp the idea that they should be invested in that stock only as long as being so is beneficial to them and the goals of their plan. That way, they can get some sleep at night, and I can, too."

You have to be very careful where you get your investment strategy education, most advisors say. "If you look at a typical cover of *Money* magazine, for example, what you'll often see is a picture of a good-looking twenty-something who has made a ton of money at whatever. You know this because he's leaning against the brand-new Ferrari he's bought, and Ferraris don't come cheap," says one of these advisors. It's true. A financial writer friend of mine, whom I promised to keep anonymous, said that the major financial maga-zine she works for has a policy of putting photos of only successful, good-looking people on the cover. "That's *not* the real world," the advisor goes on to say. "It's not any different from looking at the movie stars in *People* magazine. A lot of publications designed for consumers, including magazines on investing, just do not reflect the reality financial advisors and portfolio managers are steeped in every single day. So reach out to them for a capital education."

Education is good for everybody, advisors will tell you. The more *you* know and understand about market risk and reward, the better off you are, and the better off your advisor is.

3. Avoid Mistakes

Top financial advisors say the most common mistake new, and even experienced, investors make is to overconcentrate their portfolios

TOP FAQs . . .

Q: "Ed, how should I be investing—stocks, bonds, cash, and percentages of each—at age thirty, at forty, at fifty, at sixty, at seventy, at eighty? All the investing books I've read give me a headache."

A: "I put your question to my panel of advisors and other experts and they said that there is no such thing as a one-size-fits-all strategy for any age group. Saying so serves Wall Street, not you. It's like saying you'll need Viagra as soon as you hit age fifty or that you will have to start taking heart medication at age sixty-five. Some people will; some won't. Wall Street wants you to be a long-term buy-and-hold investor so it can hold onto your assets, when in reality, *you need to be more tactical at all ages.* Most people today who have any significant money in the market probably started investing in the mid- to late 1970s. To them, the meltdown we're seeing in the market today is an *anomaly.* They consider it normal for the market to *gain* 10 or 15 percent a year, taking them on this slow escalator ride up, whereby everybody makes money year after year. But if you go back and look at a hundred-year chart of the Dow, that's absolutely false. The real anomaly was that period of time of extreme prosperity between 1980 and 2000. In reality, markets are volatile, they're risky, they're scary, and they require professional tactical management specific to each client in order to navigate during tough times."

in one asset class and believe that makes them well diversified. This means that putting your money into, say, several different technology stocks or eight different bank stocks and thinking you are thereby spreading the risk (which is the purpose of asset allocation) is a mirage. "What you are actually doing is jumping on a particular bandwagon and basically putting all your chips on it," explains one advisor. "It comes down to this: You've been looking at whatever the best-performing asset class was, say, last year, and loading up on that class, thinking, 'Well, hey, if one of those technology companies or banks goes into the tank the others will pick up the slack for me.'

"It's true that if one stock you own suddenly underperforms while others you own stay the same or take off, you are successfully balancing risk. But it's the *asset class itself that typically falls out of favor*—like when the dot.com bubble burst in 2000 and tech stocks *as a whole* went in the tank, or when bank stocks plummeted in 2008. What worked last year is *no guarantee* to be a home run again this year or the next. It's like fighting the last war. There are statistical studies that have looked at what were the best-performing and the worst-performing asset classes every year for the past twenty years, and very seldom has there been a repeat performance; they go down *as a whole*. So even if you own shares in multiple companies, if those companies are concentrated in one asset class, your portfolio is at risk. It's a no-win approach to diversification, and bad, bad idea all around."

> *"The four most dangerous words in investing are 'This time it's different.'"*
>
> —JOHN TEMPLETON,
> founder of Templeton Mutual Funds

Advisors cite some other common investor mistakes to avoid:

- Don't be stubborn. By this they mean don't get so enamored of owning a particular company's stock, especially if you work for that company, that you can't bring yourself to part with it even if the investment plan you have put together with your advisor calls for reducing your position at some point. "Remember, investing is all about *making money*, not going for a loss," says one advisor. "For example," a portfolio manager points out, "during the 1980s and the first half of the 1990s, GE was one of the best stocks to own, ever. I had a number of clients who were still working, and some in retirement also, to whom I recommended reducing their position in their GE stock at some point to avoid overwhelming their portfolios with any one stock—even if it was GE—no matter how well it was doing or how much they admired it. They were not happy selling their GE stock. They liked being able to say they owned GE stock, but they also understood the importance of sticking to their plan. This was when GE was at fifty bucks a share. Now it's at eighteen bucks a share [in December 2008]. And none of those investors is at all unhappy that they got out."

- Asset allocation is an important discipline in investing, but by itself it can only do so much, advisors insist. "The bottom line is that investing is not just about hedging risk, it's about making money, and if you buy overpriced, overvalued stocks, you may wind up with a well-allocated portfolio but it's still a portfolio allocated with 'crap,' " one financial advisor says bluntly. "The fact of the matter is that buying the *best* of a particular asset class is always going to get you further along than asset allocation alone." It's not up to you, the investor, to recognize the best class to be in and when to be in it—or if, when, and how to shift your portfolio among them. That's your financial advisor's role. "But it *is* up to you to understand the underlying issues, to ask questions about those issues, and to heed the answers so you will stay on track with your overall strategy," he adds. "Asset allocation alone doesn't ensure a great portfolio or that you will achieve your long-range goals."

- In his book *Vince Lombardi on Football,* the legendary coach emphasized the importance of sticking to the fundamentals of the game in order to win. To paraphrase him: If you can't block and tackle, the halfback will never get out of the backfield and you will never be able to defend against a score. This advice applies to the world of investing, too. As one financial advisor commented: "If you stick to the bottom-line fundamentals of risk and reward in choosing financial products at whatever stage of your life, and don't try getting cute with a lot of complex products such as 'derivatives' or betting on the German mark versus the Japanese yen and hedging both with the Swahili whatever, you'll be able to block and tackle and come out okay. Warren Buffett, America's most successful investor, demonstrates his own block-and-tackle approach to fundamentals by never buying a company's stock if he can't understand what that company does. And it's the same with investing. *Always keep it simple.*"

4. Don't Be Shortsighted

To be shortsighted is to fall prey to the past. Shortsightedness means always looking in the rearview mirror to see what worked last month, last quarter, last year and focusing on that microcosm in your investment decisions, rather than taking in the entire financial landscape around you. What you really must do is keep your eye on what's working or not working *now*, and what markets or sectors are showing relative improvement versus which are showing some deterioration.

"It's always much more important to avoid a loss than it is to try to hit a home run—because there are not that many home runs out there to be had anymore," advises a senior investment manager. "If you're going to be a successful investor, you can't discriminate against asset classes. You can't discriminate against regions of the globe. You can't discriminate against market sectors. And you can't keep looking in the rearview mirror. You have to take the macro view."

5. Take Action in Small, Consistent Steps

It takes time to put together a really good portfolio, so don't expect to spend it all in one day, advisors recommend. This means if you have a million dollars to invest and you go to an advisor who comes up with a strategy for investing it all by, say, next week or next month, get another advisor, warns my panel of experts. All that pulling together a portfolio that quickly ensures is a really good month's worth of commissions for the advisor, they add.

Says another expert: "Truly, if you walked into my practice with a million dollars in investment capital on you to spend right now, I wouldn't do it—*couldn't do it*! It's going to take time to put together a solid portfolio because, for one thing, I'm only going to buy best-of-class assets—or try to—and that doesn't happen in the blink of an eye; it could take as much as a year, possibly."

Everything that's built to last goes together incrementally, whether it's a skyscraper or an investment portfolio. You layer everything in, brick by brick—or asset by asset. He adds, "It's kind of like when you go out shopping with your wife over the weekend. You wouldn't empty your bank account, saying, 'We've got to spend all of this today and get everything we will ever need.' You would take out enough to buy what you need for that weekend or the whole week. Okay, so maybe you also buy a few extras for fun that you really don't need—there's still going to be money left in the bank at the end of the weekend for future shopping trips. That's how to approach building a portfolio, too."

I'll leave the final word on strategic investment thinking and practices to another sage colleague who works as an advisor portfolio manager: "Most people try to construct their investments based on the day-to-day swings in the market, the latest news, the latest financial publications, when in actuality the question that everybody should be asking themselves is this: 'How do I accomplish the goals in my life that are the most important to me, with the very least amount of risk possible?' That's what people need to know. And in order to know that, they have to have a well-thought-out, well-crafted, *written* financial plan where a light bulb comes on and they say, 'I know, because of all the work that I've done that I'm set. I know that regardless of what happens in the markets, in the economy, in the world, that I've positioned myself to have the highest probability of success, of achieving the things in my life that are the most important to me, because of the choices I've made putting this plan in place.'"

SAMPLE ACTION STEPS

- Look forward, not backward, in making any investment choice.
- Get a handle on your risk tolerance.
- Allocate assets in your portfolio among different asset classes, not different companies or entities of the same class.
- Buy and sell with a result in mind—will this achieve the long-range goals of your plan?
- Strategic investing means being in the market only when it makes sense—sometimes cash or bonds are king.
- Stick to investing fundamentals—no complex, get-rich-quick schemes.

Chapter 8

THE AMAZING ROTH IRA:
IT'S *ALL* ABOUT ACCUMULATION

Sometimes one pays most for the things one gets for nothing.
—Albert Einstein

Cash-Strapped? Or Cash-Rich? It's *Your* Choice

The financial services industry and certified public accountants like myself have long advised that taxpayers choose a tax-deferred savings and retirement plan—and for good reason: For decades, tax-deferral planning has been the *only* game in town. But the advent of the Roth IRA—and now its fellow Roth 401(k) and Roth 403(b)—has changed that. Income is the name of the planning game. By paying taxes now, you will not only survive a financial storm, but you may, in fact, *prosper* (with a Roth IRA you pay *zero percent* tax on withdrawal), losing only some relatively small and short-lived tax deduction. Income that is tax free is the best income of all, since you don't have to share any of it with Uncle Sam. It's simple: When you don't have to share, you end up with more. So sharing isn't always best (just don't tell that to kindergarten teachers).

Taxes will become the single biggest obstacle to building wealth. Therefore, managing taxes is essential, especially in an environment of *rising* tax rates, which is where we are headed. This is why your retirement savings focus should be on Roth IRAs. That's the only way to get rid of the government as a partner in your savings and earnings. It's time to buy out your partner and build your savings free and clear of taxes. To my way of thinking, it's all about being tax free—moving your money from accounts that are forever taxed to accounts that are never taxed. The Roth IRA does just that.

For example, if you are in a combined 30 percent tax bracket (federal and state), a contribution of $4,000 to a traditional tax-deferred retirement plan is worth only about $1,200 in savings on your current tax bill. That's barely more than $23 a week! You probably blow more than that downloading stuff from iTunes. Remember, this money isn't a refund; it's a *deferred tax* that you *will* pay on that $4,000 contribution eventually—*plus* the tax on all the interest the $4,000 will generate over the years—when you start withdrawing money at retirement. It's like getting a cash advance on a credit card. It's great now, while you have the money, but you'll owe it all back with credit card fees and charges that will make the original advance look like peanuts. The advance is the tax refund (created by taking the tax deduction), which you enjoy up front, and the credit card charges are the taxes that will eventually be owed not only on the advance but on all the interest earned on the account. Basically, you're building a savings account for Uncle Sam. If, instead, you give up the $23 deduction for a greater reward later, the exchange is clearly much better, particularly over time, and especially since you don't have to pay Uncle Sam ever again, no matter how much you earn on the account.

Time is, after all, the greatest moneymaking asset an individual can possess, particularly a young person. Time itself is what makes this approach work, and the proof is this: 2008 marked the tenth anniversary of the creation of the Roth IRA, and ten years' worth of dollars-and-cents evidence is now in.

Here's an example: Roy started saving smartly when he was thirty-five by contributing the maximum allowable amount to a Roth IRA each year since the Roth IRA began in 1998. As of this writing (late 2008), he has contributed $29,000 to his Roth, which, after compounding at an average rate of 8 percent over the ten years, is now worth $42,719. Had he opted to contribute the same amount to his traditional tax-deferred 401(k) at work or to his own traditional IRA with the same interest rate, Roy would have accumulated the same amount of money. In addition, he would have received a tax deduction each year for his contributions. On the surface, the traditional approach seems like a better deal. But let's run some numbers.

Let's say the combined tax savings over the same ten years from 401(k) contributions would have been identical: $8,700 ($29,000 worth of tax deductions over ten years at a tax rate of 30 percent). It appears that betting on the Roth instead (as Roy did) was a poor choice. But Roy knows himself. That $8,700 in tax-deferred savings over ten years from a 401(k), which averages out to $870 per year, would be great—if Roy was disciplined enough to have invested those funds. But Roy knew that he, like most people, would probably have used that money to pay off last year's holiday credit card balances or perhaps he would even have squandered it, thereby losing every penny of his theoretical tax savings. The key here is the word *theoretical:* Many financial number crunchers will do pages of analysis to show you that if you invest that tax refund each year, you'll come out ahead. But that is just theory. Like Roy, most people are just not going to take that refund check and invest it. When I was a tax preparer, before I even finished preparing their returns clients would talk right in front of me about how they were going to spend that refund check. If the refund is going to be spent rather than invested, then the tax deduction is wasted. This throws that theory out the window. Better to forfeit the tax deduction now and live tax free later, when you'll likely need every dollar you have.

But now the *really* bad news.

If Roy had opted for the 401(k) instead of a Roth IRA, never put another dime into the 401(k), and left that $42,719 to grow for the next thirty years, at the same 8 percent average, then his $42,719 might conceivably grow to $429,867 by 2038, when he's ready to retire. But remember, *that pile of cash will not be all his:* Every dollar he will withdraw will be subject to income tax, and the rate of income tax he will pay is determined by whatever his tax bracket will be in his retirement years, which in turn is determined by how deeply in debt our government is (in other words, how much money it needs) at that time. The bigger our national debt, the higher future taxes will be. If Roy's tax bracket in retirement is 30 percent (and that is a big "if"), then $128,960 in that account will still belong to the IRS, which he will have to buy back on withdrawal. Conversely, even if Roy never puts another dime into a Roth account, that same $429,867 growth by 2038 is *all his*—bought and paid for long ago, when his Roth was worth only a fraction of that amount.

At retirement, which account would you rather have? You can see why Roy chose the *tax-free planning alternative* of a Roth IRA.

To Convert or Not to Convert

A Roth IRA might be considered the mirror image of a traditional IRA. The latter usually is funded with tax-deductible contributions, so a traditional IRA holds untaxed dollars. Distributions typically are fully taxed. A Roth IRA, however, is funded with after-tax money. You are allowed to withdraw your original Roth IRA contributions tax free and penalty free, at any time, for any reason.

Inside a Roth IRA, investment earnings are tax free, too. What's more, five years after setting up the account, you also can withdraw the earnings tax free, as long as you are at least age 59½. There are no required distributions from a Roth IRA, so you can keep the money in the account for as long as you wish. If you withdraw funds, that withdrawal can be tax free, with no impact on your adjusted gross income (AGI). After your death, beneficiaries you name will have to take minimum distributions from the Roth IRA, on a schedule determined by their life expectancy. However, those distributions also will be tax free.

You can convert a traditional IRA (where withdrawals will be taxed) to a Roth IRA (where they may not be taxed). Such conversions can be expensive, though. In essence, such a conversion will be treated as a withdrawal and taxed immediately.

Suppose, for example, you have $200,000 in your traditional

IRA and you convert that IRA to a Roth IRA. You will have to report $200,000 in taxable income on your tax return for the year.

That might not be so bad. Tax rates are at historic lows now, so you may be lightly taxed on a Roth IRA conversion, compared with the taxes you'd have to pay in the future. Once you have converted your traditional IRA to a Roth IRA, you can get started on tax-free wealth building.

Still, paying tax on a Roth IRA conversion can be painful. You might owe the IRS $70,000 in cash on a $200,000 conversion, or $175,000 on a $500,000 conversion. If you dip into your IRA to pay the tax, you'll lose some of the opportunity for tax-free buildup, and if you are under age 59½ you will be subject to a 10 percent early withdrawal penalty on the amount taken out to pay the tax. There is no penalty on withdrawals that are converted to your Roth IRA. Therefore, one tactic to consider is a series of partial conversions. Instead of converting a $500,000 IRA this year and owing $175,000 to the IRS, you might convert $50,000 of your traditional IRA per year, for ten years.

Obviously, that would reduce the annual tax obligation. Pulling out smaller amounts each year also might keep you in a lower tax bracket: You might owe 28 percent on your conversion, not 35 percent.

The $100,000 Question

Another consideration regarding 2009 Roth IRA conversions has to do with income: In the year you convert, your income can't top $100,000. The same ceiling applies whether you file a single or a joint tax return. Because of this $100,000 limit, many people have not been able to convert their traditional IRAs to Roth IRAs. That's going to change, though.

Starting in 2010, the $100,000 income cap will be eliminated. In that year and subsequent years, anyone willing to pay the tax can convert a tax-deferred traditional IRA to a potentially tax-free Roth IRA. Yes, such conversions still will be taxable. However, you might not owe tax right away. On Roth IRA conversions in 2010, tax won't be due that year. Suppose, for example, you convert a $200,000

IRA in 2010. You would pay no tax on the conversion. In 2011, you would add one-half of the conversion income ($100,000) to your regular 2011 income. In 2012, you would add the remaining half ($100,000) of the conversion to that year's income. The tax you owe for each year would be based on that year's rate. That's right—you can convert a traditional IRA to a Roth IRA and start earning what probably will be tax-free investment income right away. Yet you won't have to pay the tax on the conversion until 2012 and 2013, when you file your 2011 and 2012 tax returns. You'll effectively have interest-free loans from the IRS, lasting two and three years, during which time you can earn tax-free income.

In many situations, then, a Roth IRA can help you win the withdrawal game. After meeting the five-year, age 59½ timetable, all of your withdrawals will be tax free. If you don't need any or all of the money in the account, you can leave it there. There are no required distributions from a Roth IRA, no matter how old you are. If you leave a Roth IRA to a beneficiary or beneficiaries, they can stretch out tax-free accumulation (see Chapter 11). No matter how large the account grows or how high future tax rates might be, you and your survivors will have tax-free income. That's one way to beat the IRS in the third and fourth quarters.

Recently, the *New York Times* (October 23, 2008) reported a story about Albert Horrigan, a semi-retired real estate broker in Sarasota, Florida, who converted a $50,000 IRA to a Roth IRA in 1998. "The account grew to be worth more than $1 million," the *Times* wrote. That entire gain in his Roth IRA will be tax free forever. He doesn't have to share any of it with Uncle Sam.

Now let's explore the amazing Roth IRA from your individual perspective and see how to apply the five steps to determining whether it's right for you.

1. Know Who You Are and Where You Are

Youth has a huge financial edge here. Most people who are in their mid- to late fifties or early sixties today and getting ready to retire cannot possibly get the same wealth-building hit out of a Roth IRA as people in their thirties and forties (or even younger if they happen to be savvy savers). Savers in their fifties and sixties simply don't have as much time ahead of them—although having another twenty or thirty years of saving until they reach age seventy or eighty is certainly nothing to sniff at. Much tax-free income can be accumulated in that shorter amount of time as well.

As recent headlines have indicated, companies can take away workers' retirement security blankets in a heartbeat, leaving little more than Social Security to live on (assuming Social Security still exists when the time comes). Younger workers know, as I said in Chapter 1, that they must rely on themselves to build and preserve their retirement savings, and they should be looking for another way. The amazing Roth IRA takes the uncertainty out of how high future tax rates will rise because when you start withdrawing, every dollar is tax free (assuming you are at least age 59½ and the account is at least five years old); thus, you are assured a zero percent tax rate when you collect. Do all the projections you want, but *you cannot beat a zero percent tax rate!*

So, wherever you are along your time horizon, you can build a potentially staggering tax-free retirement nest egg, starting today, by capitalizing on (1) your age (the younger you start, the more certain the result) and (2) tax-free Roth IRA, Roth 401(k), and Roth 403(b) planning. As their names imply, these new savings vehicles combine features of the traditional 401(k) and the Roth IRA. As with a traditional 401(k), for 2009 you can set aside up to $16,500 in a Roth 401(k) account each year, plus another $5,500 if you are fifty or older. (For future years, these limits increase with inflation.) That's almost four times the amount older workers would be able to salt away in a traditional tax-deferred IRA or in a Roth IRA. But in many cases, if you have the funds to put aside, you can have both a Roth IRA *and* a Roth 401(k). That's really piling on the tax-free savings deal. The only restriction on adding a Roth IRA contribution is the income limitation. But beginning in 2010, that is easily bypassed. No, the Roth IRA contribution income limitations don't go away, but since anyone can convert to a Roth IRA in 2010 (regardless of income), you can simply contribute to a traditional IRA and then convert that to a Roth IRA.

As with the Roth IRA, Roth 401(k) and Roth 403(b) contributions go into the account after income taxes have been paid, but you don't have to pay any taxes on contributions *and earnings* when you withdraw them at retirement.

The new Roth 403(b) has also become an option for schools and nonprofits that offer traditional 403(b) plans. The Roth 401(k) and the Roth 403(b) do not have the same income limitations as the Roth IRA (where contributions are prohibited once 2009 adjusted gross income reaches $176,000 for married couples filing jointly and $120,000 for singles. These amounts also increase in future years based on the rate of inflation). As a result, many more American workers are able to take advantage of Roth 401(k)s and Roth 403(b)s regardless of how much they make, as long as their company offers these options to their existing 401(k) and 403(b) plans.

> *"Some 2 percent of 248 employers surveyed by human-resources firm Watson Wyatt indicated they have cut back on 401(k) matches as a way of coping with the sinking economy. Another 4 percent said they may join them in coming months."*
>
> —*USA TODAY*, October 29, 2008

2. Educate Yourself

For today's younger generation of savers (in their twenties, thirties, forties, and early fifties), the tax-free, not tax-deferred (i.e., *tax-infested*), approach is the future of retirement planning. Tax-deferred income plus Social Security was your parents' and grandparents' retirement plan, not yours.

The philosophy behind the tax-deferred approach is that even after paying the tax on money withdrawn in retirement there will be enough money left over to live comfortably. But that after-tax figure depends on two factors. One is the payout schedule you choose, which is predictable; the other, however, is your tax bracket in retirement, which is as yet not predictable. With the tax-free approach, you pay the government up front on each contribution you make, but your gross accumulation (including interest) remains *all yours to keep, no matter what your tax bracket or payout choice is in retirement.* The latter approach is clearly the way to live at least as long as you were able to while working and, perhaps, live even longer by having more money available to you in retirement than you had dreamed possible.

For example, children with summer jobs can fund a Roth IRA (for college, say) based on their earnings and as long as they have the money. Here is where you as parents or even grandparents can help by giving your children or grandchildren the money to contribute to a Roth IRA. You can call it their "company matching program," only it's courtesy of you. You can match their earnings up to the maximum Roth IRA contribution limits (which most young earners won't reach), and they can put that money into their own Roth IRA. Individuals can continue making contributions to a Roth IRA (unlike a traditional tax-deferred account) well into their seventies as a tax-free legacy for their children and grandchildren.

Start as early as you can, since time is the most powerful asset of all. A Roth IRA is great for children once they have earnings, no matter how small the amounts are. They add up over time. What children cannot contribute in amounts, they can make up with time, which works in their favor. Parents and grandparents should encourage their children and grandchildren to open Roth IRAs once they begin working. It doesn't matter how little they make. The important part is to get children started on tax-free saving as soon as they receive their first paycheck. Parents and grandparents can help by giving the children the money to open Roth IRAs, because chances are good that the children will already have spent most of the money they made.

I did this for my older daughter when she got her first real job at age fifteen. She worked at our local library and made all of $350 for the year. Of course, she spent that money. But I opened a Roth IRA for her and gave her $350 to contribute to that account. This gave me an opportunity to explain the value not only of saving at a young age but also of building a retirement savings account that would be tax free for her forever. None of her accumulated savings will ever have Uncle Sam as a partner.

She was trying to understand how it all worked and asked me, "Let me get this straight—I earned $350 and I spent that money . . . and then you put it back in . . . and it grows, tax free, forever? What a country! Is that the way it really works?" My answer: "Yes, while you are under this roof."

I wasn't so concerned about giving her the money to contribute. It was more important to me that she recognized the value of opening a retirement savings account and building savings that would never be eroded by taxes. I wanted to give her a start, so that when she heads out into the real world she will continue contributing to this account—with her own earnings. I believe this is more likely to happen if the account already exists.

Not only that, I wanted her to see the power of compounding and how starting young can yield exponential returns in retirement. The long-term results are incredibly powerful when you compare starting just ten years earlier to someone who begins contributing when they start their first real career job at, say, age twenty-five. Those ten additional years of compounding could be worth tens or even hundreds of thousands of dollars by the end of the first half of the game, and in a Roth IRA all of those extra dollars will be tax free, so they are so much more valuable.

Another advantage to children and grandchildren for starting early is that they begin receiving account statements in the mail. Seeing the balance increase as they (or you) make new contributions gives them that much more incentive to continue the process when they go out on their own. Not only does my daughter see the statements, but as a result of the 2008 financial crisis she has also learned about the stock market, how values can go down as well as up, and why you need to keep saving.

The Power of Ten Years

To illustrate the compounding power of opening a Roth IRA early, let's look at this simple example.

Let's say you are twenty-five years old, you just got your first job, and you are able to contribute $2,000 a year to a Roth IRA. You actually are permitted to contribute more, but because this is your first job you don't have more to contribute at this time. That's okay. It's better to start out small than to do nothing. This example is based on annual Roth IRA contributions of $2,000 (compounded at 8 percent, which is a modest return to assume over a time period of thirty years or more). Anything you add as your income increases over the years likewise dramatically increases these already impressive results.

ANNUAL ROTH IRA CONTRIBUTIONS	VALUE AT AGE 65
$2,000 beginning at age 25	$559,562 tax free
$2,000 beginning at age 35	$244,692 tax free

But what if you started at age fifteen instead of at age twenty-five? We already know that if you began contributing $2,000 a year to a Roth IRA at age twenty-five, you would have accumulated $559,562. Starting just ten years earlier, at age fifteen, gives you an additional $679,782! And starting twenty years earlier than the person who began at age thirty-five gives you an additional $994,652! That's almost a million dollars more, all tax free. The magic ingredient is time.

If you have been putting money away in a tax-deferred account all these years and want to convert (roll it over) to a Roth account, there is no limit, no cap, no ceiling on the amount that can be converted—if you are willing to pay the income tax. For example, perhaps you have a 401(k) for which your employer has agreed to match your contributions up to a certain amount, but now that amount has been reached, or your company is no longer matching contributions; the advantage of "free money" is gone, and you would be better off converting to a Roth IRA or contributing to a Roth 401(k), if your company offers that.

Here's the icing on the cake: Unlike a tax-deferred account, you never have to withdraw the money if you don't need it. With a traditional tax-deferred account, you must start withdrawing (even if you don't want to) and start paying back all that income tax after age 70½ because that's payback time for the IRS. *But a Roth IRA can grow tax free for you and your family forever.* If you are like Roy and go with a Roth IRA—or a Roth 401(k) or 403(b)—while those with tax-deferred accounts are forking over their money to the government to pay for health care and other expenses, you will be laughing all the way to and from the bank and getting ready for your tax-free vacation in Tahiti.

3. Avoid Mistakes

People are more likely to spend for a big-screen TV than to buy off the taxes on their retirement accounts. They have what I call a "spending gene." They simply have an aversion to paying money to the government because they don't see the benefit. The benefit builds over time. Especially if you are a young saver, now is the time to do it. Even if you are older and you already have a retirement account, this is something you can do for your children if you want to pass on tax-free money to them. The biggest obstacle to creating wealth in this country, no question about it, will be taxes. Those taxes could be paid now for pennies on the dollar. With a Roth account, you have a free and clear wealth-building machine that will take care of you and your family for the rest of your lives. But the psychology tends to be that of instant gratification: "I don't want to pay taxes now. I would rather buy that big-screen TV . . ." You must overcome the "spending gene" and take care of your wealth building in the short term, which will take care of you and your family in the long term.

As I've made pretty clear, the biggest mistake you can make with a Roth account is not contributing to one—or not converting your traditional retirement account to a Roth if you can. But in the event that you do go the tax-free planning route with a Roth account, and for financial or other reasons have to return to tax-deferred strategy, the Roth provisions allow you to convert your Roth savings back into a traditional IRA without penalty.

This process is called *recharacterization,* and it is another feature that makes the Roth IRA such an attractive alternative to traditional tax-deferred saving and retirement planning methods.

TOP FAQs . . .

Q: "Ed, the strategy of paying taxes on contributions now and maybe becoming a tax-free millionaire down the road is almost too BIG to get my head around. It doesn't seem doable for someone like me."

A: "You're right, it is a BIG idea. It's big because the reward is potentially immense. But it is also completely doable. Find the way that works for you. Contribute a little bit monthly, and pay the tax April 15. Or arrange with a mutual fund company to have small but steady contributions automatically taken out of your salary so that you don't feel the pain. Sure, you will have to make some sacrifices—for example, dining out twice a month instead of every week—but you won't have to radically alter your lifestyle. That would be self-defeating. Most people fail at dieting because they try to cut out everything. Just start to leverage small dollars now to get those big tax-free dollars later."

4. Don't Be Shortsighted

The big shock for tax-free planning investors, of course, is the loss of the tax break up front, but it comes as a shock only because of the conventional wisdom today that tax-deferred saving is the best available retirement planning option.

With a traditional IRA, 401(k), or 403(b), contributions are taken out of workers' paychecks before they pay any taxes on the amount of the check. That lowers today's tax bill, although Uncle

Sam eventually gets his due when withdrawals are taxed as regular income. Then, when it comes time to pay the piper, today's conventional wisdom maintains that the retiring investor will likely be in a lower tax bracket than when he or she was working. But that is a myth. Given today's huge and growing deficits, soaring health care costs, and other economic factors, such a likelihood is no longer so likely; tax rates will *increase*. They *must*—in order to keep the country from drowning in a sea of red ink. And tax-deferred investors will be paying the freight!

If you think about it, it's always the good things in life that you pay for up front and the bad things that you pay for later—and pay much more. Paying tax on your seed now so that your crops can grow tax free forever is how you create real wealth. So paying taxes now, while rates are relatively low compared to what they are likely to become, makes a great deal of long-term sense, even if there is some short-term pain involved.

The natural inclination is to follow the advice of planners who tell you the opposite—that you should always defer and not pay taxes now. That's taking the short-term view, and these planners believe that's what you *want* to hear. After all, nobody likes pain, and paying taxes, even a minimal amount, is painful. But pain is what you must endure for long-term gain. Here is what you need to think about. You can always pay later, but taking that approach doesn't eliminate the problem. Deferred taxes are like a cancer on your savings that will never go away, no matter how much chemotherapy you endure. This tax cancer just metastasizes, getting bigger and coming on stronger at a higher tax rate, until it kills your savings. Even if it goes against the ingrained philosophy of some planners and accountants (unless, like me, they're recovering ones), buy off Uncle Sam. Get his hands out of your pocket now, so you will have tax-free wealth for retirement, forever.

5. Take Action in Small, Consistent Steps

People will pay anything for a cure once they're ill, but they are not as likely to pay even a small amount to prevent themselves from get-

TOP FAQs . . .

Q: "Ed, the Roth account seems too good to be true. What if I open a Roth and the government eventually decides to pull the plug and withdraw the Roth option?"

A: "If I were the accountant for the government, I would say, 'Do not permit these Roth IRAs. We are giving the store away. If the only option offered is tax-deferred methods of savings, we stay a partner in people's retirement accounts for life.' But the government doesn't think this way. That is part of the problem. Our government is fiscally shortsighted, having no immediate cure in view. The government says, 'If we continue to allow Roth IRAs, we are going to get in a flood of money early—especially in 2010 when the floodgates open and *everybody* will be allowed to convert to a Roth under the law." So it is pretty likely the government will maintain this system. But let's say the government wises up and eliminates the Roth IRA option because it realizes it's created a legion of millionaires who will never pay taxes again. Whenever the government has ended a program in the past, it has grandfathered anyone who already participates. So I say, get in now while the getting is good! If you want to build your personal wealth tax free, you might as well take advantage of the U.S. government's shortsightedness while the opportunity is here. And by the way, I wouldn't worry about the government getting too smart too soon. Most representatives and senators won't realize there is a problem until their own checks bounce!"

ting that illness in the first place.For pennies on the dollar, you can create a plan that transforms your accumulated wealth from money shared with the government to a nest egg that is totally your own, tax free, forever. Anyone can do this, and now is the time to strike.

Bankers always advise borrowing when you don't need the money, because when you need it, they're not going to lend it to you. Retirement planning works the same way. You should do it even if you don't think you need to because you tend to be more thoughtful about it when there is no sense of urgency. Nobody is retiring or, worse, dying. You can take your time and, step by small step, work out a better plan.

Open a Roth IRA if you haven't already done so. That is a small first step toward building tax-free wealth—but it is also a major one. With that first step, you will begin to realize that every time you make a contribution to your Roth account, however small the amount, you are building tax-free wealth forever.

Little by little, you are going to wind up so far ahead of all your tax-deferred friends. Remember, the key to building wealth is keeping it out of the hands of the government. As tax rates go up—and I predict they will—the value of your tax-free account is going to go through the roof. Let's say that at retirement you've got $10 million in your Roth IRA. That's worth a lot more than a $10 million traditional IRA because a $10 million Roth IRA is worth $10 million *to you*. It's real, spendable money. It's all yours free and clear, whereas a $10 million traditional IRA will have a government mortgage on it at a percentage rate you don't yet know. That's not real money, because you can't spend what isn't yours. So taking small steps now can lead to gigantic strides later on.

SAMPLE ACTION STEPS

- Open a Roth IRA if you can.
- Determine if/when you can convert from your traditional IRA or 401(k) or 403(b) plan to a Roth IRA.
- Find out if a Roth 401(k) or Roth 403(b) is available through your job; if not, ask whether your employer could add it to your existing 401(k) or 403(b) plan.
- Maximize contributions to your traditional IRA and 401(k) or other company plan now to take advantage of the 2010 no-limit conversion opportunity.
- If you're self-employed, consider converting your SEP or SIMPLE IRA to a Roth IRA.

FYI . . .

Three out of ten large employers and about 10 percent of smaller employers are expected to add a Roth 401(k) in the next couple of years, according to surveys by Hewitt Associates and Transamerica Retirement Services. The word is spreading about the Roth 401(k) and 403(b) accounts. As with the traditional 401(k) when it was introduced more than twenty years ago, many employers will use these vehicles as recruitment tools. You should ask for them.

- Use tax-free life insurance money to raise the cash to pay your contribution or conversion taxes (see Chapter 12).
- Investigate the latest tax law changes governing Roth IRAs and the new Roth 401(k)s and Roth 403(b)s with your tax advisor, and take advantage of them.
- Determine whether you have creditor protection (see Chapter 5) for your Roth account(s).

Chapter 9
_____

INCOME FOR LIFE—WHAT'S RIGHT FOR YOU?

> I advise you to go on living solely to enrage those
> who are paying your annuities.
>
> —Voltaire, French philosopher

I'm Gonna Outlive My Money!

As I've traveled around the country doing seminars and specials for PBS, I've heard a common refrain among many of the people who attend—those who are still working as well as the retirees. It reminds me of that song from the movie *Fame,* whose chorus proclaimed, "I'm gonna live forever." Only this refrain isn't joyful—it expresses deep concern over what the prospect of such longevity could mean for them. "No matter how much I accumulate I might still run out of money and wind up in the poorhouse," they say to me. They're more afraid of going broke than of dying!

It's an established fact that people *are* living longer. Even the Hallmark greeting card company substantiates this. In 2007 it produced and sold more than eighty-five thousand birthday cards for one-hundred-year-olds. This means that not only is it possible for an individual who stops working at age sixty-five today to continue living for another thirty-five years, but they will have to do so *on a fixed income.* Thus, the prospect of running out of money to live on becomes exponentially more likely—and increases dramatically the younger you are. Young people who are now just *entering* the workforce might anticipate even longer life spans when they retire forty or fifty years from now, given the strides medical science is constantly making.

This pervasive concern over running out of cash is why I have emphasized throughout this book the absolute necessity of taking control of your own money and destiny—that is the only path to becoming secure in the knowledge that you will have income for life. Annuities are an investment option that can help you along that path. They can accomplish something for you that no other investment option can: a *guarantee* that you won't outlive your income no matter how many years you last. By taking control of your money you can pick investments that are right for you.

FYI . . .

An *annuity* is an *income* insurance product sold by a life insurance company that guarantees a series of payouts to the owner over a prescribed period of time *or* over the person's lifetime. Although offered and managed by a life insurance company, an annuity is not a life insurance policy, which pays out to beneficiaries upon the death of the policy owner. In other words, with an annuity *you* get to enjoy that vacation in the Bahamas every January, but with a life insurance policy your heirs do. (However, life insurance can be a useful retirement planning tool in the second, or winning, half of the game—see Chapter 12.) Many financial advisors recommend annuities to investors because, although earnings build, tax deferred, until withdrawal, as in a 401(k), 403(b), or 457 plan, the amounts that can be contributed to a 401(k), 403(b), or 457 plan are limited by law. There is *no limit* to how much you can put into your annuity. Also, you don't have to worry about your employer "pulling an Enron" and leaving you penniless.

1. Know Who You Are and Where You Are

Among the many reasons for taking control of your money is to be able to pick from a universe of investment options that are right for *you* and not for, say, your employer. You don't have that universe of options available to you with 401(k), 403(b), or 457 plans. But you do with an IRA, and annuities are one of these options.

At one time advisors in the financial services industry tended to look down on annuities. "Never invest your IRA money in annuities," they would say. "IRAs are already tax deferred. Why would you want tax deferral on top of tax deferral? It's like wearing a belt *and* suspenders. Who would do that?"

Today many of these same advisors are singing a different tune and now recommend the use of annuities as a great strategy for both the accumulation *and* the withdrawal halves of the savings and retirement planning game. I've had annuities in my own IRA for years, and I probably bought them at the worst possible time—at the end of 1999, when the market was at an all-time high. Then guess what happened a year later, in 2000? The technology stock bubble burst, and the market collapsed. I lost half the value of my IRA in that bear market. But you know what? If I had retired then, I would have gotten back *every cent* I ever put into my IRA because *annuities are a guarantee of that income for life.*

Furthermore, if I had keeled over dead from watching the value of my IRA take a dive, my family would have gotten back every cent I ever put in because annuities have a guaranteed death benefit. Although I don't sell annuities (or any other investment product), as a tax advisor I'm nevertheless very bullish about them, since most of my clients are not worried about running out of life so much as running out of money. Annuities can keep that from ever happening.

There are other benefits to investing in annuities, and, like so much in the financial planning realm, it depends on who you are and where you are along the accumulation-withdrawal continuum for how many of those benefits you will reap.

For example, my mother is eighty-two (as I write this). My father died several years ago, so she's a widow. But she's in great shape. She's very active, travels all over, knows what she needs, and decided that annuities could be right for her as a way to keep from ever running out of money. So she took the IRA my dad had left her and invested it all in annuities that would pay her a monthly amount, every month, for the rest of her life. She said, "If I get that check plus my Social Security every month, I'm fine." And because hers was a *fixed-rate annuity* (see step 2 description), when the market imploded in 2008 she not only continued to receive her annuity checks every month, but the *amount of those checks even went up* (for reasons I'll explain in step 3).

2. Educate Yourself

Basically, you have two different types of annuities to choose from as an investor, and the one to pick typically depends on which half of the game you are playing—the accumulation half or the distribution half.

The first is the *deferred* annuity. With this type, the money you put in grows tax deferred until you start taking it out, similar to a traditional retirement account plan. The deferred annuity is an accumulation vehicle and, therefore, great for the first half of the game, in which your objective is to build as much wealth as possible.

A deferred annuity can have either a fixed rate or a variable rate. Both are tax deferred. But a fixed-rate product (an annuity that invests in bank CDs, for example) grows at a nonadjustable rate of interest established by the underwriting insurance company. The upside of this is that even if the market tanks and interest rates drop, the value of your investment doesn't decrease because your interest rate is fixed and, therefore, your investment's value is insured. Conversely, but for the same reason, if interest rates go up, you won't be able to reap the rewards by getting a step up in your rate of earnings growth. An added downside of owning a fixed-rate annuity is that there is no adjustment for inflation, which means that if inflation is high when you start collecting, the

inflation rate plus the taxes you will have to pay on your distributions will eat into the value of your money, increasing your chances
of running out.

A deferred annuity at a variable rate of interest, however, offers
possibilities for greater and faster growth, just as a 401(k) or other
retirement account does, if the stock market goes up and earnings
surge. Plus there is inflation protection at the back end because if
the market surges, your earnings will also grow. Furthermore, unlike an IRA, there is no limit to how much money you can invest in
your annuity annually. And finally, if you happen to die prematurely during the first half of the game, the current market value of
your account's full accumulation (minus any distributions you may
have taken) will go to your family or other beneficiaries—the so-
called death benefit.

The second type of annuity is called an *immediate* annuity. It
differs from a deferred annuity in that you typically purchase it at or
near retirement; thus, it is suited to the second, or winning, half of
the game, in which everything is about income and not necessarily
accumulation. "If you have a chunk of money to put in you can
purchase an immediate annuity from an insurance company right
at retirement," says an annuity expert. "Or you can transfer the accumulated funds in your deferred annuity to the insurance company to purchase an immediate annuity. In return, the insurance
company guarantees you an income stream for life—with payments
beginning within a year [of when] the purchase is made."

Again, an immediate annuity is all about the distribution phase,
where your big concern is running out of money, and thus income,
not growth, is paramount. "If you've got a million dollars with your
broker, and your money's going down because the market's going
down, and so you're pulling money out to live on, you're in big
trouble—because the chances are, you probably *will* run out of
money," says an expert in annuities. "Now people can tell their brokers, 'Let me take some of my money and put it into this annuity
that guarantees I will never run out of money even if I live to be a
120 years old!' This is not a shot against brokers, but many of them

are just so caught up in the 'it's all about earnings' philosophy that it escapes them how important it also is to be able to *keep* what you make. That's where annuities come in. They are a guaranteed growth and income investment vehicle ideal for the uncharted waters of the day when you're on your own."

3. Avoid Mistakes

Annuities experts say not to be lulled into believing that your only option with a fixed-rate annuity is to accept inflation risk. Remember, investment and retirement planning is all about what's right for you. As I wrote earlier, my mother had a fixed annuity and yet her checks would go up at times. How could this be? The answer is that a fixed annuity can be *indexed* to offer a degree of inflation protection, regardless of whether it's an immediate or deferred type of annuity.

As one expert explains: "An indexed annuity is much different from other fixed annuities in the way it credits your interest. While as with other fixed annuities interest is credited at a set rate established by the underwriting insurance company, here that set rate is keyed to the performance of the equity index to which the annuity is tied—for example, the S&P 500 index. In other words, if the performance of the index goes up, you are credited with *some* additional interest, though not the entire upside of the return, and so your rate goes up a bit, too."

This expert adds, "How much it goes up and when you get it in your monthly check if you're already collecting will depend on other features of your annuity. But the bottom line is that with an indexed annuity, you never take a loss. The performance of the index is either added to your account if the index is up, or your rate stays where it's at if the index is down."

4. Don't Be Shortsighted

"The big knock on annuities is that they have a higher fee structure than other products and that you're wasting valuable dollars that could be better spent investing on your own in, for example, ABC Mutual Fund," says another annuities expert. "The fees are probably a little bit higher than if you were to just invest in a regular mutual fund. But you know what? *They should be—because you're getting more benefits!* You get tax-deferred growth until withdrawal. You are allowed to switch between investments in your annuity tax free. You can contribute as much as you want during the accumulation phase of your plan. And you get a guaranteed income stream for life."

This expert continues, "You don't hear many brokers claiming 'Invest in the stock market and the mutual fund companies will guarantee that as long as you leave your money there for five or ten years (depending on the companies), *you'll never lose money.*' You will lose—just as most people experiencing this latest market downturn have lost (more than 40 percent losses in many cases). It will take them ten years or more to recover from that kind of loss. An annuity is a protection against outliving your savings. You get insurance for everything else; for your house, for your car, for your life. Don't you want to insure your savings, too?"

Personally, I think so, and you have to pay for that insurance. There is no free lunch here. But the fact that you can pay extra for a lifetime guarantee of income is something you might want to consider. That's what my mom did. She simply did not want to worry about the stock market. She just wanted to know that her monthly checks would keep coming, no matter what. She wanted a guarantee of financial security, and that's what she now has. A bonus is that she no longer feels she has to glue herself to CNBC. She can enjoy classic movies instead.

So, as the experts recommend, don't be shortsighted by focusing solely on high fees and low fees. "With fees, you get what you pay for," says one expert. "But it's the added value or benefits that count, too. And from a growth *and* income point of view, these days our clients are all telling us thanks for putting them into an annuity."

"We've made too many promises and asked for too few sacrifices. We're going to have to change our culture as we know it."

—GOVERNOR DAVID A. PATERSON OF NEW YORK,
calling for reduced pension benefits because of budget problems,
THE NEW YORK TIMES, December 17, 2008

5. Take Action in Small, Consistent Steps

Annuities are now being touted by their one-time detractors as *the* modern pension plan for America's workers and retirees—especially with inflation protection added. One advisor I know who recommends and sells annuities tells me that after the crash of 2008, her seminars were filled to capacity with people seeking financial cover. She also tells me that her current clients are actually giddy about the protection they bought, while most of their friends are tearing their hair out because of the losses they've suffered in the stock market.

SAMPLE ACTION STEPS

- Open an IRA so that you can start investing in annuities.
- Make sure you thoroughly understand how the annuity works and what long-term benefits you can count on.
- If you purchase a deferred annuity, you can start accumulating now.
- If you purchase an immediate annuity at retirement, you can begin collecting income for life.
- Think benefits, not just fees.
- Consider purchasing an indexed annuity for built-in inflation protection down the road.

Chapter 10

_____

MONEY AND WOMEN

"The reason women don't play football is because eleven of them
would never wear the same outfit in public."
—Phyllis Diller

Common Bonds

Let me tell you a story that was related to me by a veteran financial
advisor who happens to be a woman and works mostly with
women clients.

For years, a woman I will call Jennie worked for a physicians'
group at a large Ohio hospital. She had just turned forty-four, when
her life took a dark turn. She and her husband of many years decided to split, and the divorce became final in January. It was then
that Jennie began experiencing a constant pain in her neck. When
she had it looked into, the diagnosis, much to her shock, turned
out to be cancer. With chemotherapy and recuperation, she would
be out of work for a year or more.

Jennie's ex had handled the family finances, so she didn't know
a whole lot about where she stood financially except that she had
benefits and a retirement plan at the hospital. Now she found herself on disability, which she could collect up to age sixty-five and
possibly beyond, but which, like most people in similar circum-

stances, she could not survive on. Furthermore, life insurance was now out of the question as an option to help with her financial situation because her cancer was considered a preexisting condition.

Most significant, Jennie had no one at her side to cook for her and take care of her on a consistent basis; her only child lived far away in another state. Nor could she afford a home health aide. So she moved back with her ex-husband, who was able to care for her mornings and evenings and came home each workday at noon to make her lunch.

Assuming that Jennie's treatment is successful and she could go back to work at the end of her long ordeal, she will not be making contributions to her retirement plan during all that time, which therefore will be losing growth and accumulation. The result: She might have to work many more years than she had ever planned on just to get by. Hers is a tragic tale all around.

Here's a very different, but equally cautionary, story shared by another veteran female advisor who handles mostly women clients.

"Hilda [name changed] was in her eighties when she came to me," this advisor related. "She had a son who lived a good distance away and saw little of him. 'He has his own life,' she told me. How often do we hear that from aging parents?

"She came to me because she was getting all these financial statements in the mail, and since she didn't know what they were or what to do with them she just kept stuffing them in a shoebox. She didn't have a lot of money and expressed concern that she would be wasting my time, but asked if I would go through the box and tell her what the statements were. They turned out to be statements for some hedge funds she was invested in. Now, hedge funds are geared toward professional and wealthy investors with gambler's blood who are willing to chance risk rather than reduce it, in the hope of scoring big. This was hardly an investment a person of Hilda's age and income needs should be making, so I asked her who her broker was. She told me she used an acquaintance, who wasn't actually a broker but worked with one. And she had given him power of attorney to move her money.

Stunned, the advisor asked Hilda how she had met this man, who was clearly doing something illegal. "She said 'church,' of course. What a surprise—it's so typical in these situations, I'm afraid," the advisor explained.

"I said, 'You know, these investments are totally unsuitable for someone your age because you can lose all your money, plus you can owe money on the account.' She was just shocked. Couldn't believe it. I asked her how her son would feel if he knew this. Her answer was, 'Oh, I would never tell my son!' So, I asked, 'If you're giving your money away like this, don't you think he *should* know?' And her answer was, 'I'm not giving it away. I mean, I'm going to ask for it back.' '*When*?' I asked. And she responded, 'Well, I don't know. I just don't know *how* to ask him for it.'

"The bottom line was, she was *afraid* to ask for her money and power of attorney back from the man she had given them to—in fact, she was afraid *of* him, a neighbor. And so she refused to act, which in her case was was very, very unfortunate."

Leave It to Cleaver

These advisors who shared their horror stories with me, both experts on the subject of money and women, maintain that while such calamitous events are not all-pervasive among women, they are regrettably not all that uncommon, either—among women of all ages, too. From observations they've made over many years of working with women clients, they explain the problem this way.

"Back in the fifties, the sixties, the seventies—the so-called era of Ward and June Cleaver—women were supposed to get married like June or become teachers, and it was *assumed* that the patriarch of the family (Ward Cleaver) would just take care of you. As a result, so many women were never exposed to dealing with financial issues, except on the most superficial and mundane level. And we're still dealing with the fallout from that," says one of the advisors.

"Now, life has changed," she continues. "As the population has aged and women statistically began outliving their husbands, we've suddenly been charged with taking care of an estate that may include large accumulations of assets [such as] retirement money, which for years had been handled by our husbands or our fathers. And to no surprise, we've run into all sorts of problems. Now we've become keepers of the checkbook and in some cases women are so completely at sea that they don't even know how to write out a check, let alone attend to larger, more complicated financial matters."

I can relate to that. I remember that when my grandfather died, my grandmother told my father that she did not need any money but she did need help paying the bills. She admitted to him that she did not know how to write a check. My dad was visibly shocked. It had never occurred to him that in all these years she had never written one.

"When women are put in that position, many times they can be taken advantage of," the advisor adds. "Because they don't know or don't think they know enough, so they sort of move around and try to find somebody whom they feel they can trust to fill the money manager role. With elderly women, the first choice is often a son, but a daughter will do if all else fails.

"More women are single mothers and so they tend to take a more personal view of money—more of an 'I'm responsible for my family' view. And they also tend to be more goal oriented and more about 'what if' than men are. They'll be more conservative and they'll want to be more protective of their finances. All of which is good, but since, in many cases, women still earn less than men, they have less leeway to work with money, and so we've found they still feel very much besieged, still feel a lack of empowerment, and still feel overwhelmed at times from being the person in charge of the M-O-N-E-Y."

Based on input from these top female advisors, here's how women can apply the five steps to becoming more financially empowered.

1. Know Who You Are and Where You Are

"Because they are so busy entering the workforce and trying to excel, taking care of their kids, and then, if a family member takes ill, it's usually they who are called upon to help out, women today still are not exposed to many financial matters until the money stops and reality hits like a brick wall," one advisor says. "They're on that wheel of life that just keeps going round and round. But then if a health care issue arises when their earning power has stopped, all of a sudden they *have* to take a hard look and ask themselves, 'Okay, what's going to be paid for? What happens if I'm ill or, heaven forbid, lose my spouse or significant other? We're living in a million-dollar house that I won't be able to keep anymore!'"

The advisor continues, "Men have a leg up because they tend to be the ones in a relationship who handle the finances. So what women must do, whether they are single, married, or in a relationship of any kind, is tell themselves they have to take time out *now* and figure out who they are and where they are financially—*before* they hit that wall, crash, and have to pick up the pieces of their lives and make financial decisions at the worst possible time."

"We'd rather give more time to getting our cars repaired than we're often willing to spend dealing with our financial life," observes another advisor. "As women, we have to face down our fear of actually taking time out to deal with this critical part of our lives. By the age of fifty-six, many of us who are married will probably be widows. That's the average age of a widow right now in the United States. And most of the life-changing events in a woman's life, according to research by the American Association of Retired Persons [AARP], happen between the ages of fifty and sixty-five. So with the year 2010 approaching and statistics showing that by then women will control 60 percent of the assets in this country, the lights need to be turned on. Women multitask in so many other areas, what's one more? Sure, the last thing we want to do at 9:30 at night is pull out our financial and benefits statements to figure out where we are. But we have to. And the determination to be able to sit down and ask questions of a financial advisor is the key to turning those lights on. It's like asking directions, which is something men never do."

When women in this difficult position finally summon the motivation to come in for help, here's how one advisor handles the consultation: "My first step is to just talk to them about their major concerns, how much they spend, how much they'll need, that sort of thing—standard fact-finding to draw out who they are and where they are because often they are so overwhelmed they just don't know where to begin." She continues, "Typically, we go over the statements and other financial records they've brought and I explain how to read them and what they are. And often there is considerable surprise that it's not rocket science, after all. I'm very open about the fact that after this first meeting I might decide there is nothing I can do for them, or they might decide they want nothing to do with me, so there's no commitment made. But if we decide to make another appointment, then what I'll do is take copies of all the statements and other financial records they've brought and put a plan together that we can talk about at our next meeting. And then I'll take things further with them. If, for example, they have variable annuities in their portfolio but don't really understand what those are, I will call up the variable annuity company, with their permission, right then and put us all on speakerphone so they can ask questions (with my prodding, if necessary). We write down whom we are speaking to and get all the information on the variable annuity directly from the company, so that when they leave my office that day they know what that investment is and why they are in it. Most important, before I recommend an investment of any kind—growth *or* income—I make sure they understand that there are fees involved, which often surprises them, too, just like finding out how much money they have or that they actually must die for their family to get their death benefits. So this first step is all about facing and overcoming ignorance."

The upshot of summoning the courage, the gumption, or the determination to take this first step is that lights will go on and doors will indeed open, the advisors maintain. "For example, twenty years ago, a middle-aged woman came to me at the urging of her daughter," one advisor explains. "Her husband had always taken care of everything, and so she had no clue what to do. She worked in a hospital gift shop, drove a beat-up Toyota, and lived in a small house with very few expenses—all because she didn't want to spend her money. When we sat down together with her statements and started listing her assets, we came to find out the estate was way over what the government would allow her to pass to her own children without a *horrendous* tax liability! She was stunned at how much she had.

"We became very close friends and she was very much involved as we worked together, planning out her future for about eighteen years until she came down with a life-threatening disease and ended up in a hospice. But we were current on everything; we had even created a trust—so that her children would receive a sizable amount when she died, and not the IRS, and to benefit the charities that were taking care of her (hospice and the American Cancer Society). And it all began with her making the decision to take the time to reach out for some answers."

> *"One who asks a question is a fool for five minutes;*
> *one who does not ask a question remains a fool forever."*
> —CHINESE PROVERB

2. Educate Yourself

The next step is to pursue some self-education so that you are not 100 percent reliant on your advisor as your knowledge base. You have been there and done that. The phrase "Don't worry, honey, I'll take care of you" is not acceptable in your vocabulary anymore. Now you want to learn enough so that you are able to make *informed* decisions in partnership with your advisors. You should never jump into making any financial decision until you understand your choices and are working from some framework of knowledge of your own.

This is particularly true if you are a recent divorcée. You are at your most vulnerable and susceptible to following advice from unreliable sources, which unfortunately often includes well-meaning friends and family members. I have seen this in my own practice and with female friends who find themselves alone for the first time in many years in their forties and fifties, raising their families, and not knowing where to turn, because this is often the first time they've had to deal with financial issues. One divorced female friend told me that she had no idea what to do about health insurance, retirement accounts, or savings in general. Someone she knew referred her to an advisor, and she did no research on her own. She was given poor advice and told to use money in her retirement account. This was not only wrong but would have triggered taxes and penalties just at the time she needed the money the most. If you educate yourself, it is less likely that you'll be taken advantage of after a divorce or other traumatic event in your life.

There are some excellent "how to" suggestions for educating yourself throughout this book that are applicable to both women and men, but here are some additional thoughts on that subject from the two seasoned female advisors, which are specifically aimed at women.

"Open your mail," says one advisor. "It may sound foolish, but many women don't open their financial statements because, in their minds, they've already convinced themselves they won't be able to read them anyway. Some will even bring in their unopened statements after they've become clients. If this is you, you're not going to educate yourself that way." I had a tax client like that years ago. She was a recently divorced single mother with two teenagers. She had a decent job, but when it came to her financial statements, she just would not—actually *could* not—open them. This went beyond a typical phobia. She would come in to do her taxes with a suitcase full of unopened letters from banks, fund companies, and, of course, the IRS. I would open the letters in front of her, and as I did, you could almost see her wince. It was as if I were sticking a pin into a voodoo doll with her likeness. This went on for a few years until she finally overcame her fear, which came about when one of the unopened letters contained a huge tax refund check for her."

In another case (this is from an actual IRS ruling), a woman lost her job but kept her 401(k) plan with that company. She should have rolled it over to her IRA so she could take control of her money, but she didn't. She didn't want to make any changes. Each month in the mail she received her 401(k) statement, and each month the balance declined. She became depressed because this was her life savings, and she simply stopped opening the mail. This went on until the next year, when she went to her accountant to have her taxes prepared. As he was going through the tax reporting forms, he uttered the familiar question (familiar, at least, to tax pre- parers): "What'd you *do*?" The tax preparer noticed that she had withdrawn the entire balance from her 401(k) plan and now owed tax and a 10 percent early withdrawal penalty on the whole amount. It turned out that in one of those unopened 401(k) state- ments from the company was a check for her entire lump-sum dis- tribution from the plan. This had to be rolled over to an IRA within sixty days in order for that money to remain tax deferred, but obvi- ously that deadline had long since passed. She filed a request for a Private Letter Ruling and begged the IRS for relief. Here's a surprise: The IRS denied her request, basically ruling that she was in control of the money and had no one to blame but herself. It was not the bank's fault or the company's fault or the IRS's fault; it was her fault for not opening the mail. And she lost her life savings.

"Many women don't want to have their grown children know what they are doing," offers the same advisor. "Unless there is some logical reason why your children should remain in the dark about your financial affairs, I recommend having a family meeting in which financial issues are discussed. You may be surprised what your children *do* know—perhaps not about your own financial af- fairs, but about the financial world in general, and you can learn from them. If it will make you more comfortable, bring in your advisor—at least initially—to mediate, explain terms, and help sort things out. This way your children can get to know your advisor, too, and be on a first-name basis with the person who is handling their mother's money." My mother, who is a spritely eighty-two, is great at this. Whenever I come over to visit, she shows me her filing cabinet full of her financial information—IRA statements, her will, her living will, her power-of-attorney documents—all in well-labeled file folders. She even had me go over her burial and cemetery plot information. She must have gotten this from her own mother (my grandmother). When my grandmother died and we went to the funeral chapel to make arrangements, I remember being amazed when the funeral director said, "It's already done. She took care of it herself. She said she didn't want to be a burden to anyone!" Of course, that's what every Brooklyn grandmother says.

"It is also true that women are less inclined than men to read books or magazines on money as a way of enriching themselves," says another advisor. "Perhaps this is because they are juggling so many other things—including making time to meet with their financial advisors—that they prefer unwinding with a good thriller or mystery than putting in 'study time.' But financial books and magazines are an educational tool that shouldn't be ignored. Streamline the process of having to search on your own for the top choices by asking your advisor for some recommendations that are both comprehensive and easy to understand." *The book you are holding is a great place to start.*

"Talk to other women and find out what they're doing in the realm of taking charge of their financial affairs," concludes this advisor. "I don't mean to ask them for financial advice or hot stock tips [a no-no to be explored in the next step]. But sharing *information* between you as you all proceed down that educational brick road is an excellent way to learn and to progress *together.*"

3. Avoid Mistakes

There are four significant mistakes about money the female advisors I've consulted for this chapter tell me women are especially prone to making and which they specifically counsel their own clients to avoid:

- "Money is like love. It's personal. It's emotional. And many women handle their money that way, instead of logically," one advisor says. "That's why they buy high and sell low—because it *feels good* to buy high. And although it feels bad to sell low, it also feels *safe* to sell low. It's an emotional reaction. They will say (and some men are guilty of this, too): 'It's time to sell off my stocks now because I'm scared about the market situation.' Maybe selling some stock *is* a right move—but the decision shouldn't just be based on a *feeling*. That's the way to make some very big mistakes." This is why these advisors counsel that when a spouse dies, for example, women shouldn't make *any* major financial decisions—or major decisions of *any* kind—just then. "They should just be taking a deep breath and letting things settle down."

- "My average client, woman or man, is seventy-three. I specialize in retirees," says another advisor. "And from my perspective about women and finance, I think women don't give themselves enough credit for being able to understand finances. And one of the biggest mistakes they make is telling people—their advisors, brokers, whomever—they can't do this, or don't know how to do that, and to just go ahead and 'do what you want' with their money. That's a sure route to being taken to the cleaners. If they have to, they should lie about it—tell people they're on the computer every day checking up. They should not be so honest about not understanding their investments and just going along 'being fine' with that."

- Don't ignore your instincts. Trust them, the advisors say. "The whole financial industry tries to discourage women from trusting their instincts," adds one advisor. "The industry just wants us to hand over our money and say, 'Do what's best.' And we're so brought up to believe that big names are better than little names—that the person who advertises most is the best—that we buy into this and tend not to trust our instincts. But if something goes wrong, women, unlike men, tend to blame themselves—because we are predisposed to accepting responsibility. Since women are more likely to watch over things that are important precisely because of their willingness to be responsible, they should sometimes apply that instinct to money issues, as well."

- "Be careful about only listening to your 'Cousin Louie,' who may say he knows everything about investments, but, in fact, he probably knows less than you've convinced yourself you do," warns one advisor. "The 'Cousin Louies' of this world just *think* they're experts. Beware of anyone bearing such 'gifts,' and you'll keep out of a whole lot of trouble."

4. Don't Be Shortsighted

Have you ever seen a broker's ad on television or in the newspaper saying "Invest in this and you'll get X percent"? Sure you have. We're bombarded with noise like that every day, and it's hard not to respond to it. But immediacy is what that noise is all about: "Everything is so good now, how can it ever be bad? So act!" It is in this shortsighted view that peril lurks—the peril that the noise may turn out to be too good to be true.

"That's why we're in this current financial crisis," says a veteran advisor. "The financial sector didn't look at leverage and risk. It was all about the noise—buy these and we'll get whatever percent more than we're getting. Then all of a sudden, they're not even worth zero percent and we can't sell them. It was all too good to be true—go for it, even if it didn't make sense to the investor's long-range objectives ten, fifteen, twenty years down the road.

"Now fear has taken over," she continues. "Women, like everyone else, are seeing the word 'recession' and hearing how it'll probably last a year, so they're letting their emotions take over and selling or doing nothing. But what about three years down the road? Will we still be in a recession? Not likely. Shortsightedness is a major issue. And women can be as guilty of it as men because they are often guided by their feelings, which can be an excellent barometer as long as those feelings don't lead to being blindsided by the short term."

5. Take Action in Small, Consistent Steps

As I've written elsewhere in this book, small steps make for great strides. This is especially true where money and women are concerned—because, as we have seen, women are often coming from behind in the financial area as earners and money managers, and in the push to catch up, there can be a temptation to bite off more than they (or anyone) can chew.

I asked the advisors we talked to for this chapter to give me their observations on the small steps that women who are in the process of coming to grips with investing and retirement planning should take.

One advisor responded, "Taking small steps in financial planning means giving yourself the ability to move around and not locking yourself into one investment philosophy or committing to one particular product for way too long a time. You have no leeway if you do that. Yes, you need to put together a plan. But understand that next year your plan is no good anymore. Because something will happen that will have caused you to do something differently over the course of that year that will affect your plan. For example, at nineteen you might name your mother as your beneficiary. But at twenty-nine you might be married and want to name your husband. Or you might be thirty-nine and divorced and want to name your children. You need the ability to make changes to your plan, and the key to that is to approach planning in steps so that nothing is ever cast in stone."

Here are the recommendations of our team of advisors:

- "Get on intimate terms with your financial statements. They are really that important, and many stockbrokers, financial advisors, accountants, and so forth, may not take the time to explain them to you. Time is money, after all. And here's a step where you can save some."

- "Involve your family, not just to learn from family members, but, especially in the estate planning area [see Chapter 13], so that family members will be aware of the wealth you have accumulated and where those assets are going, so they will know what you want and need them to do."

- "Work with an advisor who understands you, not one who is condescending and speaks to you as though, "Well, you're not going to get it anyway, so I'll just go ahead and take care of things and not bother your pretty little empty head." [For guidelines on how to avoid such advisors, see Chapter 3.]

- "Be involved. Even if you're still living at home or married and your father or spouse is taking care of the finances, understand what's going on and where things are. Don't just assume. And if you're single, understand that there's nothing in a woman's genetics that says she has no head for dollars and cents. You'll figure it out. Take it slow and steady. But *take* it."

SAMPLE ACTION STEPS

- Be proactive: If married, plan *together.* If single, don't be afraid of taking charge.
- Go over your statements until you understand what they mean.
- Do not be afraid or too intimidated to ask questions of your broker or planner.

- Beware of get-rich-quick scams and being taken advantage of.
- Have a "money conversation" with your family.
- Check with your advisor at least annually to make sure your plan is up-to-date and everything stays on course. *Don't* let this slide!

Part III

THE WINNING HALF OF THE GAME

"It's what you keep that counts."

—Ed Slott

Chapter 11

WITHDRAWAL STRATEGIES
FOR NOW AND LATER

"Recently a top NY State official who owed hundreds of thousands of dollars in back taxes offered as his excuse that he was suffering from *late-filing syndrome*. This is 'a condition that made it difficult for him to fill out his tax returns,' his lawyer said. *Late-filing syndrome*, sometimes known as *non-filing syndrome* (or *failure-to-file syndrome*), is not listed in the Diagnostic and Statistical Manual of Mental Disorders, according to a spokeswoman for the American Psychiatric Association, who added that the group does not recognize it as a psychiatric condition."

—*The New York Times,* October 23, 2008

It looks like that excuse won't work to keep the tax collector at bay. So you will need a smarter plan.

Winning the Withdrawal Game

You've saved regularly for retirement in a 401(k), a 403(b), or some other type of plan, and that may be in addition to other savings you have outside of retirement accounts. You now have a six- or even a seven-figure accumulation. In short, you're confident that you're going to be able to afford a comfortable retirement. If you're married, you believe you've provided for your spouse as well. You also might believe that some of those funds will be left over, to deliver a legacy to your children, grandchildren, or other loved ones.

Well, you're half right.

Amassing a retirement fund is only half the game. At some point—probably in your fifties or sixties or, these days, maybe never—you'll stop working and the paychecks will also stop. Then you may well have another thirty or forty years (or even longer) to live off that retirement fund you've built up. That's the second half of the game: the distribution half, when the pendulum swings and the withdrawals begin. And if you don't play well in these third and fourth quarters of the second half, you'll wind up losing—because *the IRS plays to win all four quarters.*

Some people play well in the first half, building up substantial amounts in their accounts. However, they have no plan for the second half—the half in which money is withdrawn. In fact, most people don't even come out onto the field in the second half. What's more, scoring in the first half is much easier than winning the endgame. There are many resources out there to help you succeed in the first half. Your employer probably offers a retirement plan in which you can participate, setting aside today's income for tomorrow. Many financial advisors have enough knowledge and experience to guide you through a successful plan for building wealth. But as you know from Part I of this book, that's not always the case for the second half of the game.

What could go wrong?

You might discover that the money you're withdrawing won't go as far as you expected, after you pay taxes. Thus, you might take out more money in order to meet your living expenses. Before you know it, your savings are gone, long before you are.

An alternate scenario: You could scrimp on spending throughout your retirement, denying yourself pleasurable experiences with your loved ones. This penny-pinching might enable you to leave a sizable bequest—only to have most of it taxed away before your beneficiaries can enjoy their inheritance.

Getting the best of both worlds—a comfortable retirement *and* a substantial legacy—can be done if you've accumulated a large amount of assets, including retirement savings. But to implement this profitable parlay, you have to know the rules. That's what the "winning half of the game" is all about.

As I've noted in the earlier parts of this book but which always bears repeating: The basic rule is that your tax-deferred retirement account isn't only "yours." When you get your statement and see that you have $500,000 in your account, you don't really have $500,000. That $500,000 is just temporarily on your letterhead. It is yours to share, not yours to keep. You'll be sharing it with the IRS, every time you withdraw any funds.

Suppose, for example, your account was funded entirely with tax-deductible contributions. In the jargon of financial professionals, it holds nothing but pretax money (meaning money that has not yet been taxed). That's the kind of money the government salivates over, since it is a partner in this untaxed treasure, maybe even the senior partner (meaning that the IRS may get more than you), especially when you take into account any state income taxes. If that's the case, every dollar you take out will be fully taxed, as ordinary income. Even if you sold stocks at a gain within your account, you won't get to use the favorable tax rate on long-term capital gains. Those gains will be taxed at your highest rate when they're withdrawn—the same tax rate you'd pay on interest from a bank account or your wages. Although the tax law calls this *ordinary income,* the taxes on this income are *extra*ordinary.

In addition, you'll owe a 10 percent surtax on distributions before age 59½ unless you qualify for an exception. You also may owe tax to the state where you live when you withdraw money from your retirement account. Not only that, state tax rates are increasing at an alarming rate, as revenue-hungry states go broke. Like Uncle Sam, your governor is also eyeing sources of untaxed money, such as IRA and 401(k) withdrawals, not to mention taxes on sodas, iTunes, transportation, breathing, and anything else the government can get its paws on.

Furthermore, some of you will have made *nondeductible*

contributions—funds that have already been taxed, so they won't be taxed again—to your 401(k), IRA, or other plan. If you're in that category, winning the second half of the game might be even more challenging. That's because you can't simply withdraw nondeductible contributions and avoid paying income tax. Instead, those nondeductible contributions are treated as cream in the coffee of your account. Every sip you take is taxed as a blend of untaxed cream and taxable coffee. Moreover, it's up to you to keep track of the proper proportions of cream and coffee. If you neglect to keep records, your distributions will be fully taxed—you'll wind up paying double tax by paying tax again when you withdraw money on which you've already paid tax!

Beyond income tax, your retirement account accumulation also might trigger estate tax. At your death, any amount in your IRA or other retirement accounts will be in your taxable estate. Depending on the law in effect then and your choice of beneficiary, part or even all of your retirement account might be subject to estate tax.

Even after paying estate tax, though, your beneficiary will owe income tax on withdrawals. Altogether, the combination of income tax and potential estate tax often reduces an inherited retirement account (usually an IRA) by as much as 70 to 90 percent, and that is before tax rates go through the roof as the government starts to realize that someone has to pay back the hundreds of billions in bailout money it has been putting on a credit card. That bill will come due. And who do you think will pay it? Who will bail out America? You and I, that's who! The market goes up and down and there is not all that much you can do about it. However, when the market goes back up, you can recoup whatever money you may have lost, but if you lose your money to the government, you'll *never* get it back. It's what you keep that counts at the end of the game. The taxes must be managed.

Before you begin withdrawing assets from your retirement or other accounts, you should look at all of your potential income sources. Remember that retirement funds will be taxed as you withdraw them. Other assets such as your non-tax-deferred savings ac-

FYI . . .

Just a note here: Yes, I am serious about keeping you from paying needless and excessive taxes, but I am not anti-government or anti-tax. I know that the government has to collect taxes to run our country and provide essential services. I am more in the Arthur Godfrey camp. For those of you who don't remember, Godfrey was a celebrated broadcaster and entertainer who once said: "I'm proud to pay taxes in the United States; the only thing is, I could be just as proud for half the money." I don't believe in paying *more* than you should, and I don't believe in paying taxes *sooner* than you must.

counts (these are funds you have already paid tax on) will not be taxed when you make withdrawals from them.

Minimum Distributions, Maximum Penalties

Rather than pay taxes on distributions, you might decide to keep your money in the account. If you have substantial income from other sources and you don't live lavishly, you can avoid withdrawals and the resulting income tax, right? Not really. You might think of your tax-deferred retirement account as a deal with the devil—the IRS. The deal goes like this: No, you won't have to pay tax now. But you will have to pay tax later. Even if you don't need the money, there's a required beginning date for taking distributions—April 1 of the year after the year in which you reach age 70½. Don't ask me how they came up with that date. It's a cruel April Fool's joke. Nobody knows how the age 70½ milestone was decided, either. My interpretation is that there were two congressmen in a bar one night. One was 70 years old, so he said to set the distribution age at 70. The other was 71, so he said 71. They left the bar half inebriated, slipped, and rolled down Capitol Hill, landing in a single heap at the bottom—so they split the difference and set the distribution age at 70½. Hey, it's as good a theory as any, and to my knowledge no one has yet disputed it.

Once you pass that date, you must start taking out a certain amount each year. There are some specialized circumstances whereby you could delay making withdrawals. Due to the recent financial crisis, Congress waived required minimum distributions for 2009 for IRA owners, plan participants, and even beneficiaries of those accounts. This provision may change again, so be sure to check first. This is an area about which you should talk to your advisor to get information customized to your own individual situation.

> *"Even when laws have been written down,*
> *they ought not always to remain unaltered."*
> —ARISTOTLE

The IRS publishes tables to show you the exact amount you must withdraw. In round numbers, expect to take out at least 4 percent per year when you're in your early seventies. That's about $20,000 from a $500,000 IRA. By the time you're in your late seventies, you'll be taking out about 5 percent of your IRA balance each year, and 6 percent once you're in your early eighties. And if you just say, "No, I won't take any money from my IRA," then you will wind up owing a 50 percent penalty, one of the steepest in the tax code. Say you're seventy-five years old, with a $500,000 IRA. Your required minimum distribution that year would be around $22,000. Assuming you're in a 28 percent federal tax bracket, you'd have to pay more than $6,000 to the IRS, even if you didn't need to move money from your IRA, plus any state taxes that would apply to you. Now suppose you fail to take money from your IRA that year. You'd owe about $11,000—50 percent of $22,000—just *for not withdrawing* money you didn't need. Moreover, it's probably misleading to say that you're in a 28 percent tax bracket, for instance, so the tax on IRA withdrawals is 28 percent.

The reality might be a much more painful tax bite. That's because IRA withdrawals count as part of your adjusted gross income (AGI). Many tax code provisions are linked to your AGI; the higher the AGI you report on your tax return, the more tax you'll have to pay or the fewer tax breaks you can use.

The tax return is like a pinball machine. Anytime you add income to it, all the bells and whistles go off, and anything good, such as deductions, exemptions, tax credits, and other benefits that would normally reduce your tax bill, get phased out; in the end, this increases the actual amount of tax you pay. Congress loves these phase-outs because it's a sneaky way of raising your taxes without saying it is raising taxes. But the bottom line is that you pay more, so to me that's a tax increase. Many tax professionals call them *stealth taxes,* since you don't really see them but they cost you plenty. Required minimum distributions are one of the biggest generators of stealth taxes.

For example, raising your AGI also might boost the tax on your Social Security retirement benefits. A higher AGI might reduce the medical expenses you can deduct, deductions for work-related expenses, numerous education tax breaks, and the losses you can deduct from investment real estate—and so on, from dependency exemptions to child tax credits to many other tax provisions. A required minimum distribution that appears to cost you 28 cents on the dollar may actually result in an effective tax rate of 30 percent, 40 percent, or more—and if you are in a state that follows the federal tax return, you can add on your state's cut of this stealth tax loot, too.

Okay, I guess I've got your attention by now and you finally believe me when I say, as I have throughout this book, that the second half of the game is by far the most difficult and treacherous road to staying rich for life. You have a host of potentially BIG tax problems when you withdraw at retirement. I call them the "retirement savings time bomb." What can you do to prevent them from blowing up in your face? Is it possible to win the withdrawal game? You bet. It just takes some strategizing, that's all.

1. Know Who You Are and Where You Are

Planning withdrawals is a different process for everyone, depending on how much you need and at what age you will need to begin withdrawing.

For example, if you are relying on retirement savings and you have not yet reached age 59½, at which point you can start taking withdrawals without triggering the 10 percent early withdrawal penalty, you should avoid eating into your resources. If you have already reached age 59½, then the cost of accessing your retirement savings is much lower because you will just be paying income tax on your withdrawals, with no penalties.

Then you need to know how much you have and what types of savings you have—regular savings (already taxed money) and retirement savings (funds that have not yet been taxed). You need to know your tax bracket, that is, what it will cost to withdraw funds, not only from retirement savings but from other savings. For instance, will you have to sell stocks? What other savings accounts do you have? What obligations will you face when you need to begin withdrawing? You really need a custom financial checkup before you just start taking money out.

The best way to begin a withdrawal process is to prepare a personal statement of net worth, meaning simply that you write down everything you own less everything you owe. That tells you where you stand immediately. Then write down any future obligations that you can foresee, such as paying health care expenses for your family or an elderly parent or putting children through college. By the time you are ready to begin withdrawals, which would usually be at retirement, it is hoped that your assets (everything you own) will exceed your liabilities (everything you owe). If not, then you cannot possibly begin withdrawing without a plan for increasing your income and savings. This might, unfortunately, mean going back to work, but you have to face reality. You cannot keep withdrawing what you don't have. Only the government can do that.

If your assets do exceed your debts (your net worth), then figure out how you can make that amount last at least as long as you do—and how you can minimize the long-term tax impact. Don't worry about legacies for the children just yet. First you have to have enough for yourself.

If you are like most people, you probably have the lion's share of your savings in a tax-deferred retirement account, which means there will be taxes upon withdrawal. But even other, nonretirement sources could generate taxes upon withdrawal, or they might even lower your taxes upon withdrawal. For example, you might have a regular brokerage account that was built with already-taxed money (not an IRA). But if the value of that account has increased over the years, and you need to sell some of the stock or funds to access cash, that could generate a tax as well—although it will be a different kind of tax, a long-term capital gains tax, which is generally the lowest tax rate of all. Through 2008, that rate was only 15 percent (even less in some cases). In fact, for those in the lowest tax brackets, capital gains rates could have been as low as *zero percent*. Taxes may increase, so do not count on these superlow tax rates forever; however, long-term capital gains rates have traditionally been significantly lower than ordinary income tax rates. Ordinary income tax rates are the highest tax rates.

If the stocks or funds you needed to access were sold at a loss—a scenario that is actually more common these days—then not only will there be no tax, but these losses can offset other capital gains you might have and lower your tax bill. Capital losses can also be deducted against ordinary income, such as IRA distributions, but only up to $3,000 per year ($1,500 if you are married but file separately), with the rest of the loss carried over to future years, in which they may be used. These unused losses can be carried over indefinitely, so it is important to keep track of your losses in order to use them to reduce taxes in future years.

Certain dividends (qualified dividends) that you receive on stocks and investment funds are also taxed at these preferred long-term capital gains rates, so that is another source of low-tax income that may be available to you. Municipal bond interest is tax-free income, but if you sell a bond at a profit, it is taxable as a capital gain. If the bond, like other capital assets, was held for more than a year, then the gain would be taxed at favorable long-term capital gains rates.

Rental income from real estate can be tax free in some cases when it is sheltered by depreciation deductions, but be aware that those big deductions can come back to bite you as taxable income when you sell the property. That said, rental income can provide a steady stream of cash for years, depending, of course, on location and market conditions.

The sale of a home is generally tax free if it is your residence. A married couple filing a joint tax return can exclude up to $500,000 of profit on the sale of their personal residence ($250,000 for individuals). They must have owned and used the home as their personal residence for at least two of the five years before the sale (those two years do not have to be consecutive), and they cannot have sold a home more than once every two years. So divorce anyone who might ruin this tax break for you. A surviving spouse (a widow or widower) gets to use the entire $500,000 exemption if the home is sold within two years of the spouse's death. There are more details to know about selling your home that you should get from your accountant.

The point I am making is that when you need to begin withdrawals, you can control your tax liability to some extent by knowing the different sources of cash that can be tapped at favorable tax rates, leaving you with more money. If you are not yet ready to start withdrawing, this first step will help you better plan for when that time comes. Then you will have time to change your investment mix so that you can start accumulating assets that will be taxed as little as possible when you need your money the most.

Of course, this brings us to loading up in a Roth IRA (see Chapter 8), since that money comes out tax free. Tax-free income is at the top of the pyramid. Next come capital gains rates, and then ordinary taxable income (the highest tax rates). These are the baskets you will create to carry you through your withdrawal years.

Massive layoffs have forced many workers to begin the withdrawal phase sooner than they had planned, and the market crash has left some with less than they had planned. That is why it is even more critical that the focus of your withdrawal strategy should be on keeping the most of what you have and sharing as little as you have to with the government. Often, the biggest tax savings (or most expensive tax mistakes) are the result of decisions you make when you leave your job with your retirement account. Let's cover that right now.

You're changing employers or you've put in your time, and now you are ready to retire and take your money out to live on and enjoy. What do you do? How do you seize the maximum advantage?

There are a number of choices available to you.

If your money is in a company-sponsored plan such as a 401(k), you can leave it there or move it to your new company's plan. Or you can roll it over into an IRA. You can convert those funds to a Roth IRA, if you qualify and can pay the tax. You can even take the money out now in a lump-sum distribution and pay tax. Why on earth would you want to do that? You might need the money now. Plus there are some tax breaks you can grab by taking a lump sum and paying the tax. The number one tax break is net unrealized appreciation (NUA), which is a big tax benefit if you have company stock in your retirement account. The number two tax break is ten-year averaging. To be able to take advantage of that, you must have been born before 1936, a rule that pretty much excludes all you baby boomers who are reading this. If you are going to need the money anyway (or most of it), then you may as well withdraw it and pay less tax if you qualify for either of these two lump-sum distribution tax breaks. If you do qualify, so will your beneficiaries—be sure to let them know about this.

But if either or both lump-sum distribution tax breaks do apply to you, it may pay to take the money out and pay the tax because you could end up paying much less tax than if you rolled your money over into an IRA. Funds withdrawn from an IRA will eventually be taxed at ordinary income tax rates, and those rates are likely to rise dramatically.

Generally speaking, though, your best option if you change jobs or retire is to roll your money over into an IRA, where you have better investment and estate planning options. If the value of your

IRA, in addition to your other assets, doesn't reach $3.5 million (the 2009 federal estate tax exemption amount), leaving your IRA to your children won't trigger any estate tax. Also, you can guarantee the *stretch IRA* (that great parlay of wealth I'll discuss in step 4) for your loved ones.

Leaving your money in a company plan or rolling it into a different company's plan are, I believe, the worst options because you still lack control over how your money is invested. Nevertheless, there are reasons for choosing these options, such as federal creditor protection, the ability to borrow from the plan, or, under certain conditions, to be able to take withdrawals penalty free at age fifty-five. It's a huge decision. It involves what may be the largest single check you will ever receive. So don't make this decision in a vacuum. Go to your selected advisor who has specialized knowledge in this area and seek his or her guidance at this critical stage.

Knowing who you are and where you are is essential before moving ahead with your customized withdrawal plan. Start putting together your net worth statement now to see how much you own (the three baskets of available funds) and how much you owe. Then think through how much you will need and when will you need to begin withdrawing. Pay close attention to the decisions you make when taking a lump-sum distribution from your company retirement plan when you leave the job. These decisions will impact the taxes you pay for the rest of your life as you spend that money.

2. Educate Yourself

When you enter the withdrawal stage, you need to know exactly how each source of funds will be taxed, now and over the long haul. This is especially true when you touch tax-deferred retirement savings. Remember that these accounts are infested with taxes, and you should avoid making a move that would trigger unnecessary or premature taxation of these accounts. When you move retirement money you generally get one chance to do it right—that's it, one chance! Therefore, you have to understand what moving money means so that you don't make a mistake out of ignorance and blow that one chance.

Let's say you have $500,000 dollars in your 401(k) account and you want to roll it into an IRA. There are ways of moving the money that are more advantageous taxwise than others. For example, you can take physical possession of the $500,000 and roll all that cash over to an IRA when you get around to it—just as long as you get around to it within sixty days of taking possession, or the consequences could be dire (as step 3 illustrates). But that's a bad option as opposed to moving your money via what is called a *trustee-to-trustee* transfer (also called a direct transfer or a direct rollover). With such a transfer, instead of your taking possession of the money, it actually goes directly from your liquidated 401(k) to an IRA; neither you nor anyone else ever touches the money in the transfer process. That's the surest way to move retirement money so that it's guaranteed to get where you want it to go with the least possible chance of triggering unnecessary taxes and penalties.

You also need to be educated about the tax breaks that might be available to you depending on which funds you withdraw. If you sell a stock, will the sale trigger a capital gains tax? And how is that gain (or loss) calculated? Most people who sell stocks and funds overpay the tax on those sales. That's because they use the wrong cost for calculating their gain or loss: They neglect to add the amount of reinvested dividends to the cost of their investment. As a result, they pay tax twice on the same money. Go back to prior tax returns and add up the amount of dividends you have reinvested in that stock or fund, then add that amount back to your original investment. Use that cost to determine your true gain or loss. You will be amazed at how this one move can turn a taxable gain into a deductible loss or dramatically reduce the amount of gain you will pay tax on, leaving more money for you.

Before you withdraw, you need to know how much you will keep. You should also be able to project what tax bracket your withdrawals might push you into. In some cases, retiring or losing a job could put you into a much lower bracket than before, which could open the possibility of withdrawing more and paying less in tax. Also, a lower-income year might be an optimum time to convert an IRA to a Roth IRA with a minimum amount of tax. You should be aware of these tax issues and raise them with your accountant.

3. Avoid Mistakes

The more you know about the taxation of withdrawals, the less likely you are to make costly mistakes. You should avoid withdrawing funds without knowing how much you will keep after taxes. I am not saying *never* to withdraw funds that are taxable. In fact, that could be a better move if paying the tax now is more favorable than paying much more in tax later. But you need to know this in advance. For example, I once had a client who had no idea how much the funds he had withdrawn that year had cost him in taxes, until I told him when I was preparing his tax return. I had to send out for smelling salts to revive him. This is not something to address after the fact with your accountant. The mistake is not planning ahead of time so you know what to expect—how much the taxes will be (or not be) and how much of that you can spend.

Once your money is in motion, that is when you most need to be on the lookout for tax traps that can eat up your savings quickly. The most costly mistakes usually involve moving retirement funds, since they almost always generate the largest tax bill.

The biggest mistake people make when moving their money at retirement or when changing jobs is taking possession of it with the intention of rolling it over themselves within the sixty-day grace period. Why is that such a big mistake? Here's what happens: You have to get this done within sixty days. You might think, "That's enough time. It's two whole months. I'll take the money out and move it to the IRA. How hard is that?" Not hard at all, it would seem—but in my experience with clients it's been more like *impossible* because it seldom gets done in sixty days.

The client does everything correctly and in a timely manner, but the bank makes a mistake and the money winds up in an account that's not an IRA. However, the client doesn't know this because nobody at the bank checked anything. So when is the mistake discovered? Not within sixty days, but months later, when the client comes to me at tax time, and I say, "What'd you *do*?"

The client answers, "What do you mean, what did I do? I just took the money and rolled it into an IRA."

"But it didn't get to an IRA," I say. "Now you're past the sixty days. And guess what? The money is 100 percent taxable!" That's because this money is no longer tax sheltered. Sometimes these mistakes can be fixed, but that costs even more in time and money.

A related mistake in moving IRA funds is violating the "once-per-year" IRA rollover rule, which says that you can do only one IRA rollover every twelve months. If you withdraw IRA funds in an attempt to roll them over once they have already been rolled over (within the last twelve months), the distribution is fully taxable, even if you did not mean it to be. Plus you can add a 10 percent early withdrawal penalty if you are under age 59½. This can get expensive, and there is no IRS relief for this mistake. The "once-per-year" rollover rule does not apply to rollovers from company plans to IRAs, only from IRA to IRA. So if you have rolled funds into your IRA from your company plan within the last twelve months, you can still do a rollover of those funds to another IRA.

In the run-up to the financial crisis that closed 2008, many banks were going under and people naturally worried about whether their money would get *maximum* FDIC protection, which is generally $250,000. Imagine if you had $500,000 in IRA funds. The other $250,000 would not be protected. It seems to make sense that you would roll that additional $250,000 into an IRA in another bank, thereby increasing your FDIC protection to the full $500,000 ($250,000 of protection in each bank). If you roll $250,000 over and it turns out that any of the funds from your first IRA were rolled into or out of that IRA in the previous twelve months, you just blew the "once-a-year" IRA rollover rule. The entire $250,000 you wanted to protect would then be lost to taxes, plus penalties if you were under age 59½ when you did this. Can you imagine losing an IRA of that size simply because you were taking what appeared to be prudent steps to protect that money? There is no relief for this mistake no matter how noble your intentions were. The way to avoid this is, again, to do a trustee-to-trustee transfer from one bank to the other. Unlike an IRA rollover, which can be done only once a year, you can do an unlimited amount of these direct transfers because you never touch the money.

Another classic withdrawal mistake is being made by many people right now, as a result of layoffs and the financial crisis. Many people have borrowed from their 401(k) plans thinking it is "easy money," since they have been told that the money they withdraw as a loan is tax free. Yes, it is tax free, but it is not easy money. It may be easy to access, but it still has to be paid back. If the loan is not paid back, it may turn out to be the most expensive loan you have ever taken out. It would probably be safer—and cheaper—to borrow from the Sopranos than to take a loan from your 401(k) plan, because if you default, the loan is treated as a *deemed distribution,* that is, it is considered the same as if you had taken a taxable distribution. It is, therefore, subject to tax (plus the 10 percent early withdrawal penalty if applicable). Also, you have taken a huge bite out of your retirement savings besides. This money is for later, not for now.

FYI . . .

Some companies have poured gasoline on this fire by marketing 401(k) debit cards, which can be used to instantly borrow from your 401(k) plan. Do you realize how dangerous this is? Imagine using this card at Starbucks. You thought the coffee was expensive before? Wait till you get the bill for this! To make matters worse, the card can also be used at ATM machines to withdraw cash from your 401(k). This is like giving a drink to an alcoholic. Don't borrow from your 401(k) plan, unless it is absolutely your last resort.

In a recent U.S. Tax Court case, a woman borrowed from her 401(k) plan at work, lost her job, and could not pay back the loan. Not only was the loan treated as a taxable distribution, but she also owed the 10 percent early withdrawal penalty. In addition, she got hit with a 20 percent negligence penalty (known as the *accuracy related penalty*) because the amount of tax she owed was so large. And since she went to U.S. Tax Court to fight this spiraling tax bill, she lost even more. The case took four years, and the court ruled against her. She owed all the back taxes, penalties and interest on the penalties, and those taxes for four years—on money she no longer had! So that one loan from her 401(k) plan ended up costing her not just everything she had but *more* than everything she had!

Likewise, avoid what I call "schemes and scams." These mistakes are made mostly by "sophisticated investors" (a misnomer if ever there was one) who think they can access money tax free. I see ads all the time saying something to the effect that you can tap your IRA tax free by investing in this or that. Not true. Stick with the old adage: If it sounds too good to be true, then it probably is.

These are painful mistakes, because you usually wind up paying much more in the end, what with attorney fees or IRS audit fees, plus you feel like a fool. Don't make the mistake of falling for a tax scam. The tax code is loaded with legal planning moves that you can and should take advantage of with the help of your advisor and accountant.

Whether you decide to move or not to move your money, the biggest mistake of all comes from not filling out a beneficiary form for your retirement savings accounts—unless, of course, you don't care what happens to what's left of your retirement money when you're gone. It doesn't matter what you stipulate in your will, because retirement accounts don't pass through a will—that is, they shouldn't; otherwise, your beneficiaries will end up paying more tax and paying it sooner than they have to.

Your account goes to whomever you list on your beneficiary form. That could be your sister, whom you listed thirty years ago when you first established the account. But now you have a spouse, children, and grandchildren whom you want to be the beneficiaries, but they'll be shut out if you leave your sister listed on the beneficiary form. Therefore, it's vital to complete a beneficiary form for your account and also keep it up-to-date so that it reflects your exact wishes.

What happens if you don't fill out this form and name a beneficiary? Then your account goes into your estate, to be distributed under your will. However, it will have to be distributed (and taxed) in a relatively short time period, and the opportunity to stretch tax-deferred distributions (see step 4) will be reduced.

4. Don't Be Shortsighted

This chapter has already discussed the kinds of funds you have access to and the tax bite they could incur. At first blush it might appear that you should start any withdrawal plan by taking the money that has the lowest tax cost first (such as money in your bank accounts) in order to avoid as much tax as possible. Next, sell stocks that would produce a long-term capital gain to lower taxes on those withdrawals. And last, withdraw from your taxable retirement accounts. That sounds like it makes sense, and many advisors make that recommendation. But it is shortsighted, and it may cost you dearly later on, when you are older and need to keep more of your money protected from taxes.

Take the long view on how much tax can be saved over your lifetime and beyond, not just what you can save early on. If you agree with me that taxes will increase in the future, then it might be better to withdraw *taxable money first*. That's right, withdraw your IRA and other tax-deferred funds first and pay the tax now at a historically low rate. That will put a dent in what Uncle Sam can get a piece of later—and it keeps your other (non-tax-deferred) funds growing. Furthermore, gains on those funds could even escape taxes at death.

For example, non-tax-deferred stocks or funds that have increased in value during your lifetime can pass income tax free to your heirs, but IRAs don't. Assume you own a stock portfolio (that is not in an IRA) with a basis (your original cost) of $100,000. But over the years the fund has grown to $500,000, even after the 2008 market crash. If you sell the shares to create money for withdrawals in retirement, you will pay a low long-term capital gains rate, which sounds pretty good. But if you don't touch that money during your lifetime and assume it is worth the same $500,000 at your death, your heirs will receive what's called a *step-up* in basis, meaning that they can sell the entire $500,000 of stock and pay no income tax at all. They are relieved of any income tax on the $400,000 gain. If they inherit your IRA instead and your IRA is worth the same $500,000, they will owe tax at ordinary income tax rates on every cent they withdraw. It's true that they will be able to stretch distributions on that IRA over their lifetime if you plan right (I'll get to that in a few paragraphs), but they will still owe tax on the value of the account and the earnings on the account. So think about leaving that non-IRA stock portfolio for last. Depending on your tax bracket and how much tax you can endure paying now, consider withdrawing your taxable retirement funds first and buying off Uncle Sam as the long-term senior partner in your retirement savings.

The point I am making is that you should get rid of the painful taxable money first, if you can afford to. Then look to withdraw from already-taxed money (not capital gains property). Then go to capital gains property. You should leave your capital gains property untouched until near the end because your beneficiaries will not have to pay income tax on the gains made during your lifetime. That includes your home and other investment property, but not tax-deferred savings. Leave Roth IRA funds for last. That money is simply too good to withdraw too soon.

Now on to that long-term legacy for your family. The way your family can keep building on your accumulated wealth is to make the government wait so long for its share of the pie that it can never catch up. This is what a *stretch IRA* does. I call it the "great lifetime parlay of wealth for your loved ones." And it's the best long-term planning strategy of all.

Once you roll your money over into an IRA, the option to

stretch should be automatic, but many families miss out if they do not have a proper and current IRA beneficiary designation form, or if they cannot find it when they need it—because retirement accounts should pass outside the will. However, assume that you fill out the beneficiary form. Say you leave your IRA to your son, who inherits at age forty. He will have a 43.6-year life expectancy, according to IRS tables. Therefore, your son will be required to start minimum distributions by taking 1/43.6 of the inherited IRA, or 2.3 percent. That would leave 97.7 percent of the IRA intact. As long as the IRA earns more than 2.3 percent that year, the IRA will keep growing. What's more, investment earnings remain untaxed within the inherited IRA. The next year, your son's required minimum distribution (RMD) will be 1/42.6 of the new IRA balance. He'll have to withdraw about 2.35 percent of the IRA, leaving the other 97.65 percent in the account, to keep growing, tax deferred. And so on, for a total of forty-four years.

If your son dies before the forty-four years are up, backup beneficiaries he has named (probably your grandchildren) can complete his required distribution schedule. Over more than four decades, the tax-deferred wealth buildup can be extraordinary. Assume that you leave your son a $2 million IRA, free of estate tax. Also assume that the annualized rate of return within the IRA is 8 percent. By taking minimum distributions over forty-four years, your son (and perhaps your grandchildren, too) will pull $15,871,700 from that $2 million IRA.

Alternatively, you might leave that $2 million IRA to your baby granddaughter, who inherits when she is just one year old. Your granddaughter could stretch distributions over her 81.6-year life expectancy. If she takes only the minimum required amounts and the IRA investments earn 8 percent per year, total distributions from your $2 million IRA would be $163 million!

Now add the truly magic ingredient that makes all this money tax free forever: Make it a *stretch Roth IRA*. A stretch IRA is almost as good as it gets for your family, but a stretch Roth IRA is even better. If you pass a Roth IRA under your federal estate exemption, the distributions are not only income tax free but estate tax free, too. This means that your family receives totally tax-free money for life! A stretch Roth IRA is an incredible legacy, untouchable by Uncle Sam.

Although the option to stretch is an incredible one, you first have to determine whether your beneficiaries will really benefit from it. Remember, they do not have to stretch. They could take out all the money left in your account when they inherit because they want the cash (minus all the taxes that will have to be paid at the time if they choose this course of action).

I remember years ago telling a client that by naming his then thirty-year-old son the beneficiary of his IRA, the son would be able to extend distributions over fifty years and the account would grow to millions over that time. He paused, then laughed in my face and said, "Fifty years? Really now. *My* son? Have you seen him? He's a loser. He'll have all the money spent on the way to the funeral before the body's even cold, so don't tell me about any 'stretch IRA.' He's not going to stretch anything anywhere." Then I suggested that if he really wanted to, he could force his son to stretch distributions and make them last a lifetime. And he perked up.

The way to force the stretch IRA so that your children don't blow everything you leave them right away is by naming a trust as your IRA beneficiary. But even then, if you have to force the issue, maybe you are better off leaving this child (or children) other assets and leaving your IRAs to others who are not so shortsighted and would prefer getting the benefits of the stretch IRA. After all, the only time you really need a trust is when you don't trust the person for whom you're setting it up. Maybe it should be called a "don't trust" instead.

5. Take Action in Small, Consistent Steps

By using the three biggest benefits of the tax code available in the winning half of the game, you can turn taxable money (such as your tax-deferred savings) into many times that amount, winding

TOP FAQs . . .

Q: "Ed, aside from not caring what happens to my money after I leave this world, what other reasons are there why the stretch IRA option may *not* be important to me?"

A: "Here are a few: (1) Your retirement funds are in a 401(k) and you are still working (the plan won't stretch anyway). However, there is a special provision in the tax law allowing nonspouse direct rollovers from company plans so that the stretch still may be accomplished even if your nonspouse individual beneficiaries inherit your company plan balance. (2) You are leaving the IRA to charity. The charity does not need to stretch out the distributions. It can just withdraw all the money and pay no tax, so the stretch IRA is not even an issue in this case. (3) You have only distant relatives and no close family, and you are not concerned about who gets what's left of your retirement funds. You will be spending most of it during your lifetime anyway, and whatever is left they can just inherit. They might still get the stretch IRA on whatever is left to them, but that is not a major concern of yours. (4) You feel your beneficiaries won't stretch the funds anyway, so there's no point even in naming a trust as your IRA beneficiary to try to force them."

up with more money for you now, more money for retirement, and more for your loved ones—most of it, if not all of it in some cases, tax free!

- **The tax exemption for life insurance.** You get great leverage because you can use a relatively small amount of taxable money now to have your family end up with many times that amount tax free. Plus, you have more money for yourself right now, since you have already provided for your loved ones. (For more about this strategy, see Chapter 12.)

- **The estate tax exemption.** You can use this only if you leave property (such as your retirement account or accounts) to someone other than your spouse—your children or grandchildren, for example. And if you don't use it, you lose it. Each spouse receives his or her own estate exemption. For 2009, the federal estate exemption is $3.5 million per person, so that would mean $7 million for a married couple. This exempts many more estates from federal estate tax and allows much more of your IRA or Roth IRA to pass estate tax free to your beneficiaries, who can then extend distributions over their lifetimes with the stretch option. Remember, even though your IRA passes to your heirs through your IRA beneficiary form (it should not pass through your will) it is still included in your estate. But laws change, and you need to be aware that your plan will take into account whatever the *current* federal estate tax exemption is. (See Chapter 13 for more about using this winning strategy.)

- **The stretch IRA.** Pass your IRA to your loved ones, and they can take minimum distributions over the rest of their lives, giving only crumbs to the government each year while the IRA account builds tax deferred. Make this a stretch Roth IRA by converting now, and don't even leave Uncle Sam the crumbs. You and your family keep it all. That's because you paid for the privilege up front, when taxes were on sale. Smart!

SAMPLE ACTION STEPS

- Learn account distribution rules.
- Figure your net worth.
- Understand the taxation of your different kinds of assets ahead of time.
- Have your advisor guide you in making withdrawal decisions.
- When moving money, do a trustee-to-trustee transfer.

- Look into the NUA tax break on a lump-sum distribution.
- Roll over to an IRA and name a beneficiary to get the stretch option.
- Create a tax-free legacy for your loved ones with a stretch Roth IRA.

Chapter 12

PICK THE *RIGHT* LIFE INSURANCE POLICY AND AGENT FOR *YOU*

You don't buy life insurance in case someone dies;
you buy it so others can live.
—David Buckwald, CFP, CLU, ChFC

Who Needs Insurance

"I've been selling life insurance for a good many years now," Dave Buckwald, a veteran insurance agent told me recently. "I've always believed in it, but let me tell you about an incident that made me *really* see the value of it."

He went on: "Back then I was allied with a group that handled the individual long-term disability as well as individual life insurance needs of one of the biggest brokerage firms in New York City. In fact, this firm was my biggest client—fifty-one policyholders, each of whom I handled personally; [they] were not just clients, but many of them were also my friends. On this particular day, shortly after returning from my honeymoon, I was driving into Manhattan when I heard about these two planes hitting the World Trade Center, where the brokerage firm was located. I pulled over and just hoped and prayed my clients would be all right. But things didn't turn out that way. The firm was Cantor Fitzgerald, and no one there survived, including all fifty-one of my clients. And if the planes had struck twenty-four hours earlier, I would have been at Cantor Fitzgerald myself, visiting some of them. Even now, when I look at my young children, I can't help but think how close they came to never having been born.

"Of those fifty-one disability insurance clients of mine who died on 9/11, thirty of them had also purchased individual life insurance policies from me. Many of them were young and in the prime of life, so their families were now well provided for because they had taken into account the unexpected—in this case the *very* unexpected— whereas I saw other families that day whose breadwinners had not done so, for all the usual excuses. Either they didn't want to talk about the possibility of something happening to them or they were too busy or they felt it wasn't important or that they could do better investing money on their own. And in the blink of an eye, the lives of their families had turned to *total* tragedy."

So how do *you* know whether you need life insurance? I would say you *don't* know—and that's just the point! This story may be extreme, but how many times have you read about someone you don't know suddenly dying young—like the actors Heath Ledger and Bernie Mac—or someone you *do know* dying unexpectedly in their thirties, forties, or fifties? After getting over the initial shock, it's natural to wonder whether their families have been provided for.

The traditional reason to buy life insurance is to protect your family financially in the event that something happens to you. But a second powerful reason is *wealth transfer.* Life insurance is by far the most effective way to leverage your wealth during your lifetime and for the benefit of your children, grandchildren, and other family members, and even your favorite charity, after you are gone.

The tax code allows you to buy significant amounts of life insurance to accumulate more money for yourself during the first half of the game *and* to keep your accumulated assets intact from taxes during the all-important winning half of the game. There's a massive— and growing—pension and health care crisis in this country that the government and baby boomers (the largest demographic in the history of the world) are only now beginning to pay attention to. The longer they live, the more scared people become that they're going to run out of money. Life insurance can offer new hope to you and your family for staying rich for life.

1. Know Who You Are and Where You Are

If you are reading this, you probably want to be financially able to provide for those you care about. Only you know what kind of financial security is adequate for yourself and your family, but there is no question that the most tax-efficient and cost-effective way to guarantee that financial security at any age is with life insurance. When it comes to life insurance you should think big because of the leverage. The fact that you can turn small amounts of tax-free income into large amounts of tax-free cash makes this a wise long-term financial move. Most people who have life insurance wish they had bought more when they could. No matter who you are or where you are, regardless of age or stage of life, life insurance should play a part in your family's overall financial plan. Here are the basics of how it works.

When you take out a policy on your life, you name a beneficiary, who will eventually collect the death benefit. That death benefit will be free of income tax. Even if only $10,000 has been paid in insurance premiums and the death benefit is $1 million, no income tax will be due. Let's say you start withdrawing $3,000 every year from your retirement savings as soon as you're 59½ and can do that without paying any penalties. Of course, you will have to pay income tax on the withdrawals; after paying that tax, you'll probably net $2,000. It's also true that you'll have less money in your retirement account if you take out $3,000 a year.

But let's say you go ahead anyway and use the $2,000 you net each year to buy insurance on your life. That simple strategy will likely produce a far more ample payment for your beneficiaries at the end than will the savings you did not withdraw. Depending on your age, gender, health, and the type of policy you select, they might receive anywhere from $125,000 to $500,000! Furthermore, they will receive that guaranteed six-figure life insurance payout *free of income tax,* whereas an inherited traditional retirement account would remain taxable. (It is true that Roth IRA payouts will be tax free. However, if you had a Roth IRA in the preceding example, the $3,000 you withdraw each year would be tax free, so you could put more into life insurance and thus generate an even larger death benefit.)

What's more, if you leave your retirement savings account to a beneficiary other than your spouse or leave it to charity, the balance will be subject to estate tax as well. That doesn't have to be the case with life insurance proceeds, and depending on the size of your estate, this could be of huge benefit to your family.

One tactic is to withdraw money from your retirement account, pay the income tax, and give the after-tax amount to your children. In 2009, you can give up to $13,000 to any number of recipients, free of income tax. This is called the *annual exclusion gift* (see Chapter 13). Then your children can apply for a policy on your life and pay the premiums with the money you've given away. If they own the policy, the proceeds won't be included in your taxable estate.

I can almost hear you questioning this strategy: "Wait a minute. Did you just say to take money out of my IRA and pay income tax before I am required to?" Yes, that is right. I believe that tax rates will skyrocket and you need to start moving your money from taxable accounts to tax-free accounts if you want to keep it. The Roth IRA is one way to do this, but doing this with life insurance is much more powerful because of the leverage (the ability to turn small amounts of money into huge tax-free payouts), plus you are providing a guaranteed tax-free death benefit to your family if you should die prematurely.

I advised in Chapter 8 that it pays to convert your IRA to a Roth IRA and pay tax now, and the same is true in this case. If you agree that tax rates will increase substantially, then it pays to buy out Uncle Sam as the senior partner in your retirement savings as soon as possible and put that money, and the guaranteed growth (the death benefit), in a place where the government can never touch it.

You really have no choice, since you must begin withdrawing

from your tax-deferred retirement accounts (but *not* Roth IRAs) after reaching age 70½ anyway. So why wait? Do it now while taxes are low (remember, they are on sale now)—unless you are not yet 59½ and would incur a penalty.

I am not suggesting that you go broke putting money into life insurance. Obviously, you still want to live, but if you have funds sitting around in an IRA or other savings that you don't need to live on, then those funds are better off growing tax free with life insurance than sitting in a savings account that's building for Uncle Sam and not your family.

More, More, More

"With life insurance you'll have *more* money to enjoy now, *more* for your retirement, *more* for your loved ones, and *more* of it tax free!" When I mention this in my seminars, the crowds go as wild as they do in sports arenas. But a little while later, some people look at me in confusion and ask, "What's in it for me? How does life insurance give *me* more? Where's *my* More, More, More? I drop dead, and everybody gets paid. To me, that sounds like *less, less, less!*"

Here's how *you* get *more.*

An elderly couple will come to me accompanied by their adult (often forty- to fifty-year-old) children. They will sit down at the conference table with me and proceed to tell their offspring how much they have sacrificed to give them a better life. "We didn't own big houses, with big mortgages," they'll say. "We didn't have fancy cars. We walked uphill to school, and uphill back. We didn't have expensive shoes; we didn't have feet. We had nothing! We haven't even eaten for thirty years so that you could have a great life. And the reason we are here today with Mr. Slott is because we want to continue not eating for the rest of our lives so that you can have it all." Okay, maybe I'm exaggerating—but not by much! I call this the *martyr syndrome*—the self-imposed restrictions that keep people from enjoying their own money.

Let's say you have a net worth of $1 million, but you can't bring yourself to spend any of it because you think you have to save it for your kids. Why not just peel off 5 or 10 percent—who'll know?—and put that into a life insurance policy. Your kids will have millions more than you ever had, and it will all be *tax free,* so they're taken care of and you can enjoy the 90 or 95 percent that is left. You can eat again! It's okay to enjoy your money. Be like the guy who said, "I spent 95 percent of my money on wine, women, and song—the rest I squandered!" The life insurance allows you to remove those self-imposed restrictions on your own money. You earned it, and now you can enjoy it because you no longer think you have to sacrifice to save money for your children. That's how *you* get More, More, More.

Here's a story about two of my clients who got More, More, More by including life insurance in their financial planning. I hadn't seen this couple, who were in their sixties, in a while. In fact, when I checked their file, I saw that it had been twelve years since I had worked on their estate plan with them. They came in for an update. I first reviewed the recommendations I had made twelve years previously, which included purchasing life insurance and long-term care insurance, changing ownership of assets between husband and wife, checking their beneficiary forms, and a number of other items that I have also advised for you and your family throughout this book.

I asked them what they had done so far. Incredibly, they had done everything I'd recommended, which is *not* the case with most people, who seldom follow through on much of what their advisors suggest and thus end up with the government plan. This couple were the perfect clients. At this point, the wife got a little teary-eyed and broke down, saying how thankful they were that they had followed through on my recommendations. She wanted me to know that both she and her husband were ill—terminally ill, in fact. But because they had done everything right, they were able to enjoy the time and money they had *and* still know there would be plenty of money left for their children, grandchildren, and all the other people they loved. They could enjoy every last penny of their accumulated wealth and still have peace of mind, knowing that there would be plenty left. They truly had More, More, More—and so will their loved ones.

As you can see, this strategy assures your children of receiving a large amount of cash, tax free, at your death. At the same time, it can help you enjoy a comfortable retirement. That's because you won't have to worry about saving money for the next generation. You'll know that your kids will have a substantial inheritance from the life insurance. Therefore, during your lifetime you can spend down your assets. If you're married, you and your spouse can cash in your bank accounts, your brokerage accounts, your mutual funds, and so on. You can sell that vacation home you no longer use and spend the sales proceeds on a cruise with your grandchildren.

As with winning the first half of the game, the younger you start, the better off you will be. The more you accumulate, the more you can leverage to buy life insurance and win big-time for yourself and your family.

2. Educate Yourself

"There are fundamentally five types of life insurance," explains an expert financial advisor and insurance agent. "The first is *term insurance*. It's the simplest, most straightforward, and least expensive type of policy to buy. It is appropriate for people who may not make a lot of money but need a lot of coverage because they're just starting out accumulating wealth and have a young family. So they buy term insurance for a set period [thus, the word *term*] of ten, twenty, whatever number of years to pay a specific lump sum to their family in the event something happens to them like suffering a permanent disability or premature death. The death benefit and the policy limit are the same—a $200,000 policy pays a $200,000 death benefit. It is pure insurance with no bells and whistles."

The other four types of life insurance are more expensive than term insurance because they provide not only a death benefit but also a savings element called a *cash-value account* within the policy itself. "These savings elements are wonderful because they can be used to grow money tax deferred like a 401(k) or other retirement account, but much better because they can be accessed tax free," this agent says. The other four types of life insurance are:

- **Whole life**

- **Variable life**

- **Universal life**

- **Universal variable life**

Each falls into the category of "permanent insurance," the agent explains, because unlike term insurance, which guarantees insurance protection only for the period set by the policy, these others guarantee insurance protection over the course of your whole life. That protection ends only when you do (unless, of course, you stop paying the premiums, which is how the insurance company makes its money).

    Which type of permanent insurance policy is right for you and best suits your individual asset accumulation, protection, and estate planning needs? The expert I consulted describes each one, how it works, and what it does for you within the framework of this book.

- **Whole life:** This pays a death benefit to your beneficiary and offers you a low-risk cash-value account and tax-deferred cash accumulation. The rate premium is locked in when you buy the policy, and it can't increase during your lifetime as long as you continue to pay it. The insurance company manages the cash-value account in your policy, allowing you the option to either receive dividends or apply them to reducing your payments. You also have the option to withdraw money from the account in your policy for any reason during your lifetime.

- **Variable life:** Like whole life, this pays your beneficiary a death benefit and also offers you tax-deferred cash accumulation. Your premiums are higher, but more of what you pay goes into your cash-value account, allowing the death benefit to go up depending on the returns of your account. As a policyholder, you thus have greater flexibility (more control), but at more risk. You also are able to borrow from the policy during your lifetime.

- **Universal life:** Here the earnings in your cash-value account are tied to short-term market interest rates. Those market rates can go up or they can go down. There are no guarantees. But you have greater premium flexibility about the additional amount of money you can put in than you do with either whole or variable life. There used to be no limits, but over the years the IRS has imposed certain limits on how much you can contribute, which are based on your age, your health, and other factors that go into making the calculation. Again, you have the right to borrow or withdraw money from the policy during your lifetime.

- **Universal variable life:** This gives you more control over your cash-value account than any other permanent insurance type of policy by offering you separate accounts to invest in, such as money market, stock, and bond funds. There is a stipulation, however, that if you terminate it in the early years of the policy, you will receive less cash-value total return. As with the other three types, you can make withdrawals or borrow money from the policy throughout your lifetime.

3. Avoid Mistakes

A top insurance agent related this story: "An older fellow came to me accompanied by his grown daughter, who was his beneficiary, and said, 'I've got a $40 million estate I'm trying to leave. Is there anything you can do for me?'" You're probably thinking, "$40 million! I can't relate to that!" Think again and keep on reading, because this story isn't about numbers, it's about planning.

"I told him he had an estate tax problem that would probably wind up losing his daughter half the assets he wanted to leave her," the agent continued. "But there's a way to use life insurance to create money to pay the estate tax without losing a dime of the estate," he added encouragingly. Nevertheless, the old guy just shrugged and said, "Who's going to give life insurance to somebody like me, who's terminally ill with cancer?" And the agent replied, "Well, you never know. You see, at the end of the year many insurance companies have a quota to fill, so they will insure even some risky cases at that time." Since the year was, in fact, coming to a close, he picked up the phone and called several companies to see what they would do. Two of them came back with offers to take the terminally ill man's policy. One offered a $20 million policy (that would cover the estate tax) for a one-time payment of $5 million, which the multi-millionaire could easily do. "I thought he would be thrilled," the agent told me. "But he looked disappointed, almost as if I'd called his bluff. He glanced at his daughter, who said, 'I think we should check with some other experts and study the offer.' I replied, 'What's to study? It's on the table and gives you what you need.' But they decided to think it over.

"Three months of stonewalling later, the man died. His daughter, who had been the chief obstacle because of her insistence on studying everything, called me and asked what she could do now. I told her to just make out a $20 million check to the government because there was no leverage now to do anything else. They had had an excellent opportunity to use life insurance to preserve the estate, but they blew it. Missing out on such opportunities is one of the biggest mistakes you can make."

Life insurance is a great way to really build tax-free wealth by turning taxable money into tax-free money over a long period of time. Many people understand this, but then make a mistake with the policy itself. I've encountered this mistake many times in talking to thousands of consumers at my public television seminars: Almost nine times out of ten, they own the policy in *their* name. "Why would you want to own something that you can't possibly collect on?" I ask. In response, I always get a look that says, "Are we missing something here? Maybe there *is* a way we can collect on it." The answer is no. Once you're dead, you're dead. You can't reach out and collect anymore—not even in the Hereafter.

Nevertheless, I still get the look: *There must be a way!* Believe me, there is no way. That's why you shouldn't own the policy in *your* name—if you do, it goes back to your estate when you die. And if your estate is subject to estate tax, you've cut Uncle Sam in for up to half. Although life insurance proceeds to beneficiaries are income tax free, they are not automatically estate tax free; however, you can arrange it so they are, by *not* owning the policy in your own name.

Why do so many people make this mistake? Generally, they do so out of ignorance—theirs *and* their insurance agent's. Most everybody who buys life insurance buys it from an agent who sells it to them. Some insurance agents can be as under-educated in this area as the clients they serve; they are just out for a quick sale. This is why it is so important to pick a savvy agent who really knows his or her stuff (see step 5).

Here's the way to avoid making this mistake: The agent should know and inform you that life insurance should be owned outside of the estate, particularly if you want your children or grandchildren as beneficiaries. They should own the policy, either in their own names with you as the insured, or, if they're young, it should be kept in trust (see Chapter 13). The premiums are paid either by the owners of the policy, who are your children or your grandchildren, or by the trust, and they pay the premiums with money you give them each year within the gifting limits. This way, when you die, all of the life insurance comes out estate and income tax free. In addition, your estate is reduced by the total amount of the gifts you have made to them to pay the premiums (see Chapter 13). If you withdrew retirement funds to make the gifts, then the amount of taxable retirement funds in your estate is also reduced. Your family will receive not only more money but more of it tax free, and the higher tax rates are at that time, the more valuable that money will be.

"Make today pay off tomorrow."
—WALT DISNEY

4. Don't Be Shortsighted

Life insurance means paying now for a benefit later—*much later,* you hope. As with anything else worthwhile, you pay up front for a future benefit, so you cannot be shortsighted here. You need to take the long view.

TOP FAQs . . .

Q: "Ed, leveraging life insurance is a good idea, but it costs too much."

A: "Wrong way to look at it. What's the greater cost going to be later on when the money you could have accumulated from such leverage will really count, either for use in retirement or for your beneficiaries when they inherit? What will it cost not to do it?"

For many, the tax benefits of life insurance appear too good to be true. How can the government afford to give the store away and let life insurance money be collected tax free? With the government needing so much money these days, won't it take away the tax exemption for life insurance? I get that question at almost every seminar, and my answer is *no.* The exemption will stay in place for three reasons (not counting the insurance lobby, which would be a fourth reason):

1. The U.S. government keeps this exemption because it knows that most people will be shortsighted and not use it—that people tend to focus only on the short-term cost and not the tax-free windfall they would receive later.

2. As I wrote in Part I of this book, our government is broke. It can't afford to help anyone anymore—especially you (unless, of course, you can prove that you are too big to fail with a government bailout). Why do you think that our government encourages us through tax deductions to give money to charity? So that

it doesn't have to! The more we give, the less the government has to pony up and the less of a burden that puts on Uncle Sam. It's the same thing with life insurance. Our government *wants* us to use life insurance to help take care of our families, so that it won't have to take care of them.

3. I don't know for sure that this last reason is true, but it is certainly believable. Insurance advisors and others have told me over the years that more than 80 percent of our senators and representatives use the life insurance exemption themselves. And it is unlikely that our legislators would wipe out a goodie that benefits them.

For all these reasons, I wouldn't worry about this great tax break going away anytime soon. So don't be shortsighted. Take advantage of it now.

5. Take Action in Small, Consistent Steps

I am hoping that by this point I have at least interested you enough to take some action, even in small steps, which I know will lead to major accomplishments later. So it's time for you to talk to a qualified insurance professional, or several of them.

In Part II, I walked you through the step-by-step process of picking a financial advisor, attorney, and accountant who will be right for *you*. This process is no less important when picking an agent to help you with your insurance planning. Having gone through the first four steps, you have now arrived at the key moment when you need an advisor to guide you and successfully implement your insurance plan. Take it slow, ask questions, and, above all, cross just one bridge at a time. Here's how to do all that.

There's an old joke told by insurance people that goes something like this: A potential client comes into the insurance agent's office and says, "Good morning, I wonder if . . ." And the agent jumps from his chair, hand outstretched, and interrupts: "What you need is a $_____ variable life insurance policy. Oh, did I get your name?"

The point of the joke is that this agent is not an advisor but a salesperson, and definitely *not* the type of agent you or anyone interested in insurance would want.

So what should you look for in an insurance agent?

As with other kinds of advisors, professional designations are important indicators of competence and expertise, but they are not the be-all and end-all. "I'm a certified financial planner, a chartered financial consultant, and a certified life underwriter," says this highly credentialed veteran. "That doesn't mean if someone doesn't have designations they're not any good. I know some who are very competent, but as a general rule, I think designations show that you take the business more seriously—because you have gone to the trouble, and expense, of getting education and passing tests. So it's not a hard-and-fast rule, but certainly a guiding one."

The second thing to look for is personality, he says. "What I mean by that is not to look for someone who is all charm and 'on' all of the time," he explains, "but someone you take an instant liking to. Life insurance is not a one- or two-year proposition. This person could be the insurance advisor you're going to be dealing with for the next thirty or forty years. There's got to be some degree of confidence and rapport there at the start."

The third, and perhaps most important, guiding principle of all, he explains, is to choose an insurance agent who doesn't represent and sell the products of just one insurance company. "There are a lot of good companies with a lot of good products, but those products are not always the best for all situations," he says. "And there are a lot of agents working for companies who are brought up in an atmosphere that only their company's products are best, so they will try to make those products fit you any way they can. The company's products may indeed be great, but if they're not suitable, they're not suitable. You want an agent who can and will walk your side of the street and not just that of the insurance company he or she works for—and who is able to offer you a selection of the best products *for you*."

To give you an idea of how insurance fits in with an overall estate plan (see Chapter 13), let me tell you a story about clients of mine, a couple in their sixties—the typical age when most people begin taking action in this area (though I am hoping that more young people will start looking into life insurance after reading this chapter because they can really benefit from this strategy).

The couple has a forty-year-old daughter. They have accumulated $1 million in their IRA. They have a house, but not much else. The first thing I asked the wife was "Do you love your daughter?"

"Of course I love my daughter!" she replied.

"Okay," I continued. "I just wanted to make sure. Here's what I suggest: Change the beneficiary on your husband's IRA from you to your daughter. This way she will get it estate tax free, since it will pass through the estate tax exemption. And since she is much younger than you, she will be able to extend distributions from the IRA over her lifetime, and she will end up with millions—all estate tax free! How does that sound?"

"Over my dead body!" she said.

I threw a little gasoline on the fire by asking, "What's the problem?"

"Are you kidding me?" she exclaimed. "That's all we have. We worked our whole lives for this money."

Egging her on, I responded, "But your daughter will have millions and have it for life, so what's the problem? I thought you said you loved your daughter? That's why I asked you that."

"Yes, I love my daughter, but *I want the money*!"

"What money?" I asked.

"The IRA. I want that $1 million," she said.

In case you're wondering, the reason I pressed her on this point was to get the woman (or her husband—either one of them would do) to tell me she wanted the money so that I could address a big misconception, which is that she and her husband believed the IRA is real money. It isn't.

"You don't want the IRA—that horrible, disgusting, tax-infested account," I told her. "That's not *real* money. There's a mortgage on that. Most of that is owed back to the government. Plus you have to take required minimum distributions on that money after you reach age 70½. Income taxes could be 50 or 60 percent or more on that money by the time you reach in for yours. You'll pay the most tax just when you're the most vulnerable. That's the government plan. You want to take control of your money and your *financial security* [which actually meant more to her than money]. That's where life insurance comes in," I explained.

"You said you want $1 million," I went on. "Okay, so we'll take out a $1 million life insurance policy on your husband, for pennies on the dollar. When he dies, you will receive $1 million in life insurance, all tax free. That's *real* money—free and clear and spendable. It's all yours with no taxes, no restrictions. And your daughter will get the IRA and have the opportunity to make the government wait for its money. How does that sound?"

"But where are we going to get the money to pay the premiums?" she asked.

"From the IRA that is going to your daughter," I replied.

"Oh. Well, that's okay," she said, and her husband nodded. (I thought he'd fallen asleep.)

"When your husband dies, you will receive $1 million tax free . . . and your daughter will receive whatever is left in the IRA after paying the premiums and living expenses," I added. "You should deny yourself nothing. Whatever your daughter receives is gravy. All the while you are paying premiums, you are really paying nothing—you are investing for the long run and moving your money from *forever* taxed to *never* taxed."

Then the wife said, "But what if it turns out I need the IRA money, too? Who knows what I will need, with this economy?"

I answered, "If that might keep you up at night, let's do this instead. Keep the insurance policy, but let's change the beneficiary of the IRA back to *you,* the way it was originally. The only thing I would add is to make sure that when we switch back we add your daughter as the contingent beneficiary. Now when your husband dies, not only will you receive the tax-free $1 million worth of life insurance, but you will also receive the $1 million IRA. You will have everything and be in control of all the money. You will have total financial security. And because you were smart enough to name your daughter as the contingent beneficiary, you have up to nine months after your husband's death to 'disclaim' [refuse] all or any part of the IRA, and it goes to your daughter. So you each get the best of both worlds, and you have really milked the tax code for all it's worth."

That's how you get More, More, More.

SAMPLE ACTION STEPS

- Leverage your assets with life insurance to accumulate more wealth for you and your family during your lifetime.
- Leverage your wealth with life insurance to turn taxable assets into tax-free assets.
- Use the annual exclusion gift to purchase life insurance.
- Buy permanent, not term, life insurance protection for taking advantage of cash-value accounts.
- Put policies in the names of your beneficiaries so that you do not own them, keeping them out of your estate.
- Seek maximum customization and flexibility from your insurance product *and* your insurance agent.
- Look at the long-term, big-picture benefit of life insurance and take advantage of the life insurance tax exemption.
- Use life insurance to create financial security (real money) for your spouse and your loved ones.

Chapter 13

ESTATE PLANNING BASICS

Money isn't everything but it sure keeps you
in touch with your children.
—J. Paul Getty

When I do estate planning with clients, they often phrase their questions this way: "If I die, what will happen to . . . ?" And I always jump in to correct them. "Excuse me," I interrupt. "It's not *if* you die, but *when* you die." I know that by saying this I am leaving myself open to accusations of seeing dead people. But I have done a study to support this conclusion, and that study confirmed that three out of three people do die.

What Would Happen if You Died *Tomorrow*?

Many people associate the word *estate* with the superrich or the elderly. But that is a misconception. An *estate* is your accumulated wealth—everything you have built up in the first half of the game that you own (less whatever you owe). In other words, it is your *net worth*. And *anybody* who has accumulated almost any amount of assets has an estate. If you are a young person building a 401(k) plan, you have an estate. If you are in your twenties and you and your young bride have just bought a home, you have an estate. So having an estate can apply to anyone with some financial worth—even if it's a bank savings account.

> *"It's just paper—all I own is a pickup truck and a little Wal-Mart stock."*
> —SAM WALTON, Founder of Wal-Mart

Estate planning is all about what happens to those assets (where they go and to whom) if you die *today*. Although we may prefer to believe that estate planning is something to be dealt with at some far-off point when we've got all we're ever going to have in life, the uncertainties and unpredictability of life mandate that you confront this issue no matter where you are along the accumulation-distribution continuum—that is, *if* you want to win the second half of the game for you and your family.

Nobody knows what's in your mind unless you communicate it. That's what estate planning does. It gives direction about how you want your estate to be handled, specifies to whom you want your assets passed, and sets it all down in legal terms so there's no confusion. Without this written communication of your intentions, the likelihood is that a mess will follow.

Leaving clear instructions is a must for all your property, regardless of taxes or the property's financial value, including items that have only sentimental value like family photos, letters, diaries, or articles of clothing. Let your wishes be known.

And think about this: What will happen to all your e-mail when you die? Most people, but especially younger people, have all kinds of personal information out there in cyberspace. That's property, too, even though it has no financial value. Wouldn't you want a say in who gets access to it after you're gone? In fact, this was the subject of a recent court case involving a young Marine who died in Iraq. His parents wanted to retrieve his e-mails as a memorial, but the late soldier's Internet service provider (in this case, Yahoo!) refused, until the parents got a court order.

Most people assume that if they're married, everything will automatically go to their wife or husband. That may be the case, but given the statistics on divorce and remarriage and the number of offspring from multiple marriages in this country, you never know who might turn up to lay claim to your assets, so is that really an assumption you wish to make?

And then there is the situation of unmarried partners. Unmarried partners don't have the legal remedies available to them that married couples do. This makes it all the more critical for unmarried partners to specify their intentions through estate planning—whereas in most states your assets would normally go to your spouse if you died without writing out your intentions, the same might not be true for same-sex partners or heterosexual couples without a marriage license.

Depending on the size of your family, typically the more assets you accumulate, the more detailed you should be about what goes where and who gets this or that amount. Furthermore, different types of property in an estate should be passed in different ways to ensure the outcome you desire. For example, you can pass your estate through a will, or you can set up some form of trust to distribute your estate according to your wishes, giving you even more control. As you will remember from Chapter 11 and elsewhere in this book, for the best results your retirement account(s) should be passed via a beneficiary form and kept out of your will.

The bottom line is that you should set up your estate plan so that your accumulated net worth passes to your heirs in the simplest, most efficient way. This means less chance of family squabbles and other adversarial problems, less chance of involving attorneys, less chance of people coming out of the woodwork to make a grab at your assets. Every one of these possibilities can mean that less of your money goes where you want it to go and more of it goes into the pockets of the courts, lawyers, and other professionals who will have to be hired to figure out what your true wishes were. I'm just guessing, but I think that you probably wouldn't want the details of your estate clogging up the courts for years, as in the case of the estate of the legendary soul singer James Brown. An April 24, 2008, article in the *New York Times* described the subsequent confusion this way: "After the self-proclaimed 'hardest-working man in show business' died on December 25, 2006, a welter of lawsuits emerged involving his children and grandchildren, people who claim to be his children, his wives, and women who claim to be his wives, each seeking a piece of the singer's estate." The courts are still trying to figure out the Brown family tree!

It's Not Just about Estate Tax

Another misconception many people have about estate planning is that it's only about saving on estate taxes. This might have been true when the estate tax exemption (the amount that can pass tax free) was about $600,000. Even back then, some folks who owned houses worth more than that wondered how they would pass them on without having the government become the biggest beneficiary.

As a case in point, one of my clients came in for an estate plan

FYI...

When I use the phrase *estate tax exemption,* I am referring only to the *federal* exemption. Many states have decoupled from the federal estate tax system and created their own, often much lower, state estate tax exemption amounts in order to collect more estate tax because they need the money. For example, in New York, if you die with an estate of $3.5 million, you will pay no federal estate tax, but since the New York estate exemption is only $1 million, you could pay over $250,000 in state estate taxes. So depending on where you live (or, I should say, die), you might have to plan for state estate taxes. Any experienced estate attorney will know the amount of your state's estate tax exemption, but be sure to take it into account in your estate planning.

checkup late in 2008. We had already prepared an estate plan for him and his wife about ten years previously, when the exemption was $600,000 and his accumulated worth was a little over a million dollars. In creating that plan, we had separated his property, putting some of it in his wife's name and some of it in his name, so they could each use their own $600,000 exemption to avoid estate taxes should either or both of them die that day. Ten years later the estate had grown to $3 million, so he and his wife were naturally concerned about estate taxes. But they didn't have to be, because in 2008 the exemption had grown to $2 million for each of them, and it increased to $3.5 million in 2009.

Most Americans today are like this couple. As the estate tax exemption has gone up, fewer and fewer families face the prospect of paying estate taxes. As a result, according to a recent article in the *Wall Street Journal,* fewer people are filing estate tax returns anymore.

Estate planning today is more about what you want to accomplish than about just eluding estate tax. Still, taxes are an issue. As you will recall from Chapter 1, the realities of our Y.O.Y.O. economy indicate that *income* taxes in the future are going to go through the roof, so one of the major goals of estate planning now is to keep your net worth as far away as possible from triggering huge income taxes when the estate passes. Most people's single largest asset will be their retirement savings account—be it a 401(k), an IRA, or whatever. Without some thoughtful estate planning beforehand, *all* of that money will be subject to income tax when it passes.

FYI . . .

Yes, taxes need to be planned for, but they should not change your choice of beneficiary. You should not name beneficiaries just because it might be better taxwise. *Name the people you want to be your heirs, and then do the planning to make sure that those people inherit with the best possible tax plan.*

1. Know Who You Are and Where You Are

When clients come to me for help with estate planning, we begin by figuring out who all the key players are—in other words, we put together a *complete* family tree.

This first step is all about opening up, and that is why it is often easier to involve an advisor or professional mediator than to fly solo with family members—especially if there are some black sheep among them or in cases where spouses of grown children are concerned. Many of my clients have said that it's not their children they worry about, it's whom their children marry. ("I've earned all this money, and I'm fine with it going to my daughter but not to that scalawag husband of hers.") You might have that concern as well and want to create a plan with more postdeath control, perhaps including a trust to make sure that property stays in the family.

In identifying all the key players, it is important as well to explore the family dynamics. Who gets along with whom? Who doesn't get along? Who is good at managing money? Who is bad at it? Who are the spendthrifts, and who are the savers? This last question reminds me of an exchange between a taxi driver and his fare. "Your son tips much better than you do, sir," said the taxi driver. "That's because he has a wealthy father. I don't," said the fare.

Are there elder family members who may not be as well equipped to handle the money you wish to leave them? Do you have young children? If so, who do you want—and not want—taking care of them after you're gone, and how?

Taking stock of these conditions helps the advisor to determine, for example, whether a trust (and trustee) are needed to look out for heirs, such as underage children, to make sure they're not taken advantage of or can't squander their inheritance. Another issue to examine is whether there is a family business. If so, you should identify the players and how *they* get along—or *don't* get along.

These are the things I try to find out when determining who clients are and where they are with regard to family. In many ways it's like the vetting process undergone by the president-elect's cabinet appointments in a new administration. I want to know what might come out of the woodwork, such as kids from prior marriages or former spouses. There must be *no surprises.*

Then I want to identify all the client's assets and, of course, where those assets are located. It may emerge that the client's accumulated wealth includes up to ten different retirement accounts. This might sound extreme, but it's not really all that uncommon these days. Perhaps having all these accounts spread around is a paperwork headache (and potentially a logistical nightmare), so it would be better to consolidate them and simplify the client's life as well as the estate plan. After all, ten accounts means ten monthly statements, ten quarterly statements, ten year-end statements, ten tax reporting statements, and a bunch of 1099s at the end of the year. It's like having a house full of stuff—your goal is to thin things out and make it easier and more efficient, not harder and more complicated, for the next generation to inherit. The last thing you want is to send your family on a treasure hunt. That kind of adventure can turn expensive, and ugly, very fast.

TOP FAQs . . .

Q: "Ed, by taking care of this aspect of my life and creating an estate plan now, am I jinxing myself into an early grave?"

A: "Many people feel this way. They don't want to do an estate plan because of the superstitious belief that if they do, they'll die. Well, I've got some earth-shattering news. If you *don't* do an estate plan, you'll still die. But you'll die leaving a big, fat mess, and your family will hate you forever!"

2. Educate Yourself

If you are unmarried (a widow or widower, single, divorced), planning is essential to make sure your funds go exactly to the people you wish. For married couples, if one spouse dies, then even with poor planning, property will probably end up with the surviving spouse. For unmarried people, however, there is no such thing as an "automatic" beneficiary, so you have to make sure that you name the people you wish to inherit your savings and other property.

If you are an unmarried couple (or domestic partners), planning is essential, since blood relatives may have greater rights to your property than your partner if nothing is specified otherwise. Planning can also prevent post-death problems such as relatives who contest property that you wanted to go to your partner.

Same-sex couples who are legally married under state law are not entitled to the tax benefits married couples have under federal law. Under federal law, for example, while married couples can generally leave each other unlimited amounts of property tax free at death under the marital deduction provision of the tax code, that deduction is not available to a surviving partner. Furthermore, a surviving partner cannot do a spousal rollover if she or he inherits your retirement account, the way a married couple can. So it is extremely important for you to name your partner specifically for all property that you want to pass to him or her (since the partner will not have the spousal benefits and protections that married couples have under federal law, even in the case of a same-sex couple who are legally married under state law).

Types of Assets That You Own

Everything you own at death is included in your estate for estate tax purposes, but that does not necessarily mean there will be an estate tax. As already noted, only if the value of the estate exceeds the current federal exemption of $3.5 million will it be subject to federal estate tax. So most people will not have to pay this tax.

But when you leave property to beneficiaries, even if it is estate tax free, they might have to pay income tax—on withdrawals from inherited retirement accounts, for example.

There are basically two types of property included in your estate: property that receives a step-up in basis and property that does not. It is important to understand the difference so that you know which assets of yours will be subject to income tax upon your death and which won't.

Property that receives a step-up in basis is not subject to income taxes after your death, since your beneficiaries inherit this property at its current value as of the date of death. If they sell it for that same value, there will be no income tax to pay. The date-of-death value is their new cost for determining any taxable gain or loss when they eventually sell the property.

Here's an example: If you bought your home twenty years ago for, say, $100,000 and it is worth $1 million at your death, when your beneficiaries inherit, their cost (their basis for tax purposes) is stepped up (increased) to the $1 million value at death. If they sell that home for $1 million, they pay no income tax on the sale. The step-up in basis eliminates the income tax on the appreciation during your lifetime. If your beneficiaries sell the home later on for more than $1 million, they pay tax only on the amount over $1 million. So if they sell it for $1.4 million, they will pay a tax at the long-term capital gains rate on a profit of only $400,000, since their cost was $1 million. The property does not have to be held for more than one year to receive the favorable long-term capital gains rate, as property sold during your lifetime does.

This step-up in basis is one of the best tax breaks in the tax code and applies to most of your other assets as well, including stock, collectibles, and other estate property that appreciates in value. Unfortunately, however, retirement accounts such as IRAs, 401(k)s, annuities, money or wages owed to you at death, and other, similar property, which is known in the tax code as *income in respect of a decedent* (IRD), do *not* receive a step-up in basis, and the untaxed gains will be subject to income tax when withdrawn by your beneficiaries.

Let your beneficiaries know that if they do inherit an IRA or other IRD and the estate is also subject to federal estate tax, then they are entitled to a special income tax deduction for the federal estate tax paid on that IRA or other IRD. This can be a very large tax deduction and is often missed by IRA beneficiaries and their accountants.

Roth IRAs are likewise included in your estate, but your beneficiaries will not have to pay income tax on those distributions because you have already paid the tax during your lifetime when you began contributing or converted your traditional IRA or company retirement plan funds to a Roth IRA. (Good move, by the way!) Similarly, life insurance proceeds are income tax free to your beneficiaries and can also be estate tax free if the policy is not owned by you, which is why I am such a big fan of life insurance (see Chapter 12).

Depending on the post-death income taxes and when they are paid by your beneficiaries, those who receive property that gets a step-up in basis receive more because they don't have to pay any income tax on that property. They keep it all. That is something you may want to consider when planning which beneficiaries will receive which types of property. That can all be made easier if you just leave each of them an equal share of all your property. I mention the income tax issue in case, for example, you want to leave a retirement account to one beneficiary child and a house of equal value to another. The one who gets the house gets more, since he or she gets it income tax free.

How Property Passes to Beneficiaries

There are two ways that property passes to your beneficiaries, depending on how your property is titled. One way is through your will (for property held in your own name), which means it goes through probate and can be time-consuming and expensive, depending on how clear the provisions of your will are. Wills are also public information and can be contested. The other way, which is generally better, is by having assets that are legally spoken for—that is, they have a named beneficiary—such as joint accounts, IRAs, other retirement accounts, payable-on-death accounts, annuities, and life insurance, pass via a beneficiary form or by operation of law, thereby avoiding the will and probate. Assets held in a revocable trust also pass outside of probate according to the terms of your trust, with no questions asked.

Don't interpret what I said about having your property not pass through your will as a reason for not having a will. You still need a will to execute other personal wishes, such as taking care of minor children; paying debts and expenses; leaving tangible property like a car, artwork, or collectibles; or making specific or charitable bequests. Wills can also include trusts that are created under the will to pass property. Wills are still the tool for stating your wishes and intentions.

Types of Beneficiaries

Whom should you name as the beneficiary of your accumulated wealth, including your retirement savings accounts? Answer: The people whom you want to inherit those assets.

For IRAs and other retirement accounts that do not receive a step-up in basis and are subject to income tax when withdrawn by your beneficiaries, the types of beneficiary and how they withdraw will determine how much income tax they will pay and how soon they will pay it. Your beneficiaries need to know about this.

The following beneficiary information applies solely to IRAs and other inherited retirement accounts, but that may be the bulk of your estate. If it is, then make sure you and your beneficiaries have at least a basic understanding of what to do when they inherit these accounts.

Here are your IRA and other retirement account beneficiary choices:

- **Spouse beneficiaries:** This means husbands and wives.

- **Nonspouse beneficiaries:** A nonspouse beneficiary is any person who is not your spouse, such as a child, grandchild, parent, grandparent, friend, partner, niece, nephew, cousin, or any other person (it does not have to be a relative).

- **Multiple beneficiaries:** If you have more than one IRA beneficiary, which is very common (for example, you might have three children), then you need to know about *splitting the IRA* in your estate. Either you take care of this during your lifetime or you advise your beneficiaries to do this after you die. The reason for splitting the accounts into properly titled separate IRA accounts (where your name remains on the account forever) is so that they can each stretch (see step 4) distributions based on their own (younger) age and (longer) life expectancy.

- **Nonhuman beneficiaries:** No, I'm not talking about vampires or the living dead but beneficiaries such as *estates, trusts,* or *charities,* which have no life expectancy like a living, breathing son, daughter, or spouse do; thus, distributions will have to be taken sooner after death, usually resulting in higher income taxes.

    - ***Estate as beneficiary:*** Sometimes people name their estate as beneficiary of their IRA in the erroneous belief that they are essentially naming their family. But this is a costly mistake (for reasons detailed in step 3); nevertheless, it happens frequently as a result of negligence and ignorance.

    - ***Trust as beneficiary:*** There are two basic types of trusts: *living* and *testamentary.* Living trusts are drafted and implemented while you, the owner, are still living. Testamentary trusts are drafted while you are living, but they commence at your death. These two basic types of trusts are further divided into two subcategories: *revocable* and *irrevocable.* With revocable trusts, you, as the owner, have the right to modify or cancel the trust and remove or substitute property while you are alive. Irrevocable trusts, once in force, cannot be changed and no asset assigned to them can be recovered. In addition to living trusts and testamentary trusts, there are *bypass* trusts, *charitable* trusts (remainder, remainder annuity, and remainder unitrusts), *credit shelter* trusts, *grantor* trusts (retained annuity, retained unitrusts, and retained income), qualified terminable interest property (QTIP) trusts, and more. If you and your advisor decide that the best move is to leave your IRA to a trust, the trust must qualify under the tax rules. If you want your trust beneficiaries (most likely your children or grandchildren) to be able to stretch distributions they receive from the trust over at least the lifetime of your oldest trust beneficiary, you'll need to work with an attorney who is a specialist in IRA trusts (see Chapter 4); otherwise, what your beneficiaries will inherit is a nightmare.

- **_Charity as beneficiary:_** If you are charitably inclined, a charity is the best beneficiary for your retirement savings because it pays no income or estate tax. The strategy here might be to leave your human beneficiaries non-IRA or other retirement account money instead and leave your IRA money (which is loaded with taxes) to your favorite charity.

FYI . . .

Name both primary and secondary (contingent) beneficiaries. Contingent beneficiaries will inherit if the primary beneficiary dies before you, the estate owner, or if the primary beneficiary disclaims (refuses) his or her inheritance, so that it can pass to the named contingent beneficiary. Think of the contingent beneficiary as a backup plan—a Plan B.

3. Avoid Mistakes

Here are some of the biggest mistakes to avoid.

Although all of your property should be included in your estate and is supposed to be spoken for in your will or on your beneficiary form, items sometimes "grow legs," as the saying goes among estate planners. This means the estate owner wants to leave the item out of the estate and pass it another way besides through a will.

Here's an example. A woman came to me for estate planning and during the consultation she told me she had an expensive collection of porcelain statues that she wanted to leave to her grandchildren, but she wasn't going to put them in her will. Instead, she had stuck a piece of tape to the bottom of each statue with the name of the grandchild it was intended for on it. But at a family gathering at Christmas, when she had all the grandkids over, she caught one of her daughters switching the names. That's when she realized she had made a boo-boo.

What could she do? One solution—laborious as it may be and more than possible to forget—would be for her to check the bottom of each statue every time the family came over and reinstate any names that had been moved. A simpler solution that would also ward off disagreements would be to give the items to the grandchildren while she's still alive. This option would also allow her to enjoy the looks of joy (or disappointment) on the grandchildrens' faces when they received the bequest. A third option, of course, is to leave the statues to them in her will and name the beneficiaries. If you want your assets to go to specific people, be specific in your will. Do not name your estate as the beneficiary, hoping the assets will get to the intended people anyway. You will only have turned them from non-probate assets into probate assets, and probate is a time-consuming and costly process that can be contested. There is also a chance that an unintended beneficiary could wind up inheriting assets you didn't want him or her to receive. Furthermore, an estate has no life expectancy, so anyone who inherits through the estate loses the ability to stretch an inherited retirement account over his or her lifetime (for more about this strategy see Chapter 11).

When it comes to retirement accounts, the biggest mistake is not naming a beneficiary or not being able to locate the beneficiary form after death (which may amount to the same thing). As discussed elsewhere in this book, it is the beneficiary form that determines the ultimate value of that retirement account and how soon the post-death taxes have to be paid by your beneficiaries. If you have retirement accounts, the beneficiary form is the single most important estate document.

Another mistake regarding documents is not having a durable power of attorney in place, so that if you become disabled or incapacitated, someone you trust (very much!) has the power to make financial decisions for you, pay your bills, file tax returns, transfer funds, and sign legal documents in your place. You should also not neglect to provide health care instructions if you anticipate not being able to make medical decisions for yourself. Documents such as health care proxies, advance medical directives, and living wills should be addressed, in accordance with your beliefs. But whatever your wishes in this area, let them be known in writing.

A common mistake made by many married couples is not taking advantage of each spouse's estate tax exemption. If they don't use them, they lose them. For example, in 2009 each person gets to pass $3.5 million free of federal estate tax, so a couple should get $7 million of protection, but they often don't because they leave all their property to each other. If your combined estate is well under $3.5 million, this is not a big issue. But if it exceeds or will exceed that amount, you probably should structure your property and estate plan so that you maximize the available exemptions. You can do this by leaving property to someone other than your spouse or by creating a credit shelter trust whereby the property remains in the trust, which pays income to the surviving spouse after your death and is included in your estate rather than that of the surviving spouse.

Those who own a business should have a succession plan in place, so it is clear who will inherit the business and keep it going. If you are in business with partners, it is a big mistake not to have such an agreement with them. What happens when a partner or shareholder dies? Do you want to be partners with that partner's spouse? Possibly not. There should also be a buy-sell agreement to pay off the family of the deceased partner—perhaps funded with life insurance (see Chapter 12). Make sure to let your family know if people or business associates owe you money, whether it be loans, back rents, mortgages, business receivables, or other debts. Your beneficiaries must know about these owed assets so that they can collect them, otherwise the assets could easily get lost in the shuffle. If you owe money, that is not as big a problem, since most creditors will find their way to your estate. But it should be clear in your estate plan which beneficiaries will pay which debts so that the decision doesn't wind up getting made in the courts.

> *"The large print giveth, but the small print taketh away."*
>
> —TOM WAITS, singer-songwriter

4. Don't Be Shortsighted

A couple came to see me to set up an estate plan for a multi-million-dollar estate. Before they even sat down, the wife said to me, "We have to finish this in an hour." I told her that was not possible, given the size and complexity of the estate issues involved, and I asked her why this had to be done so quickly. Her answer astounded me. She replied, "I just put a quarter in the parking meter and we only have an hour. I don't want to have to put another quarter in."

If any one aspect of staying rich for life calls for looking at the big picture and taking the long view, it is estate planning. *This is especially true for younger people, who often act as if they are immortal.* They are told that they should take care of this, but somehow they never get around to it. You might think that you have no money to speak of, but maybe you have some assets that are even more valuable than money—young children, for example, or a spouse or other loved ones whom you want to provide for. One of the best ways to really get a long-term bang for your buck is with your retirement savings. Since your retirement accounts are generally subject to income tax after your death, there is planning that can be done to make sure they last not only as long as you do but for the lifetime of your children and grandchildren. I am referring, of course, to the concept of *stretching* the distribution of your retirement savings, which I mentioned in Chapter 11.

5. Take Action in Small, Consistent Steps

The toughest part of getting started is, well, getting started. That's as true for estate planning as it is for every other subject covered in this book. Likewise true is the old adage that "a job begun is already half done." Doing nothing is, of course, a plan, but it cedes control of your assets to the government. Is that what you want?

People make all kinds of excuses for doing nothing. Here's one of the most amazing, in my experience. An elderly woman of about eighty came to me at the behest of her fifty-year-old daughter to discuss estate planning. The mother was worth millions. She was also a widow with no siblings or other offspring, so her one daughter would inherit everything. I suggested that she start gifting the assets to her daughter now. The estate tax exemption was a lot lower then, which was a problem, but she could seize an advantage by using the annual gift exclusion—the amount ($13,000 in 2009) she could pass to her daughter each calendar year without any tax consequences—and start reducing the size of her estate. Right in front of her daughter, the woman said, "I can't give money to her. She'll just spend it. She can't hold on to money. She doesn't know what to do with it." The daughter looked shell-shocked. "Ma, what are you talking about?" she responded. "I've always been good with money!" To which her mother replied, "What about that time you were in Alaska? Remember, you bought me that salmon and had it shipped? Remember how much you paid for that? I could have gotten it at the fish market down the street for one-tenth of the price. You just throw money away." The daughter looked at her wide-eyed, jaw practically on the floor. "But, Ma," she said, "*that was thirty years ago. I was nineteen and was only buying you a present from the cruise I was on!*"

As William Faulkner wrote, "The past is never dead, it isn't even past." Regrettably, this poor woman's mother lived by that. She dug her heels in, shot down my gifting suggestion, and decided to do nothing, letting everything pass to her "spendthrift" daughter in its own good time through the estate. When she died, the estate was worth even more millions—and the daughter wound up paying a fortune in estate taxes. It's ironic that the woman thought her daughter threw away money: The daughter had spent only a few dollars on a fish, but Ma turned it into a million-dollar salmon!

The first thing to do when creating an estate plan is to decide to address the issue in the first place. Talking with your loved ones (and for some of you, that might even be your family) is the best place to start, especially if yours is one of the all-too-common situations in which there are multiple marriages, stepchildren, and grandchildren involved. It is even more important to take action if you are single, widowed, or divorced to ensure that your wishes are carried out. That's why you need to think about who your executor or trustee (if you set up a trust) will be. That person will be personally liable for making sure things go as you plan. Therefore, you must likewise be sure the person you select is competent, educated, responsible, and up to the task. When there's money involved, there is a good chance of a lawsuit after death if your beneficiaries contest the actions and decisions of your executor or trustee. When that happens, the lawyers become your beneficiaries. As I like to say at the close of my estate planning seminars, "When should you do this? Three words: *While you're breathing*."

Once the estate plan is completed, make sure that your loved ones know where everything is, that personal identification numbers (PINs) and passwords for online accounts are written down somewhere, and that all your bank and property records can be accessed after your death. Remember: As long as you're alive you can continue to make any changes you want to your estate plan at any time. At one of my seminars, an elderly man came up to me and said it was his understanding that he could not change his IRA beneficiaries after he reached age 70½. I don't know where he got this idea (from his beneficiaries maybe?), but it certainly is not the case. When I finally got across to him that he could change his beneficiaries at any time, he smiled and said, "Oh, now I get it. That means I still have leverage." I asked him what he meant, and he replied, "I just turned eighty a few weeks ago and had a big celebration. Two of my kids didn't show, so they're out!"

In addition to the tools and strategies I have already covered in this chapter, here is one final technique that may be less well known but is extremely effective in solving estate problems, reducing taxes, and doing some good. It involves charity. Now, your first reaction to this might be that you don't want any of your property going to charity because it's all intended for your family and other loved ones. But the beauty of this strategy is that it can benefit both. In fact, most people who employ it are not charitably inclined at all. They just want to make sure that everyone gets more, with the exception of Uncle Sam, who has to eat the bill.

This tool is called a *charitable remainder trust* (CRT), and it has become very popular for passing assets in an estate and keeping them safe from taxes, especially where there may be substantial capital gains involved. I asked a colleague who is an expert on trusts of all kinds to give me an example of how he has employed this tax-saving strategy for the benefit of one of his clients. His story shows how a CRT can be used effectively to limit estate and other taxes while providing increased lifetime income for you and more for your beneficiaries to inherit—and help a charitable cause to boot.

"I have clients—husband and wife, both retired teachers, ages seventy-four and seventy-two," this colleague told me. "Years ago they bought a home where they worked in California. It cost them about $300,000. That property is now worth $5 million, just because of the Silicon Valley boom in property values. They also have a million-dollar IRA and about $2 million in stocks and bonds. And they're just retired teachers, mind you, not the superrich. When I met them they were working with some other advisors— one for their IRA, another managing their bond portfolio, and so on—but they had no one to really look at the whole picture. So I said to them, 'If the two of you were to walk out of here today and get hit by a car, your family [they had four children and eight grandchildren] would be stuck with paying a huge estate tax bill, given the overall size of your estate plus the value of your IRA.' Short and simple, $3 million of their $8 million estate would go to the IRS and each of their four kids would wind up with roughly

$1.2 million—out of which they would have to pay income tax on the IRA. So, in effect, this couple's biggest asset, their $5 million home, had actually turned into an estate tax liability. And if they were to sell the house (which they wanted to do so they could move to a retirement community) there might be a whopping capital gains tax. What to do?

"I recommended they look at a CRT. Here's why: Their cost basis (original price they paid) on the house was, as I've said, about $300,000. In addition, they had made $700,000 worth of improvements over the years, so their new basis was $1 million, plus the $500,000 that would come off tax free under the home sale exclusion, for a total basis of $1.5 million. So, if they sold the house, they could take out $1.5 million tax free. But that would leave $3.5 million subject to a combined federal and state capital gains tax of almost a million dollars. Then, what's left after income taxes would still be in their estate and subject to estate tax at death, leaving the government with more than their beneficiaries when added up. But if they transferred the house to a CRT and sold the house on the open market as trustees of the trust, at the close of escrow two checks would be cut. One for $1.5 million (the return of basis), which would come out of the CRT tax free to the couple. The other check would be for $3.5 million, the balance of the $5 million selling price. That amount would stay in the CRT, avoiding 100 percent of the capital gains tax. It can be invested for growth and income by the couple in the CRT because as trustees they have full control over that money, plus income for life. The charity itself doesn't even have to be made aware of the sale as long as it is named in the trust document. The charity is not involved at this stage."

The result of this CRT strategy is that the capital gains tax on the sale of the home is avoided. My colleague continues, "An income tax deduction is generated by the transfer of the house into the CRT. Then, after death, estate tax is reduced because the asset is no longer in the estate. They end up with more control over their asset than if they had to change ownership to avoid taxes. They have also increased their annual income substantially, since they are receiving income from the funds inside the CRT. That income can then be leveraged into life insurance. Often this life insurance can be for many times the value of the property when it was originally put into the CRT. This leaves the beneficiaries with a significantly greater inheritance and more of it tax free, and they do not have to deal with the property in the estate. They have tax-free cash, which is as good as it gets. And guess what? Even though they were not originally charitably inclined, the charity benefits, too. Everyone wins. Using the annual gift exclusion and other strategies, they could reduce the size of their estate and save even more —but one step at a time."

SAMPLE ACTION STEPS

- Know what your net worth is and how you want your property to be distributed after your death.
- Determine which property will get a step-up in basis after death and which property (such as IRAs) will be subject to income tax when your beneficiaries take distributions.
- Know which property will pass through your will (and be subject to probate) and which will pass through by beneficiary designation or by operation of law and go right to your named beneficiary or joint property owner.
- Sit down with your family and address your estate plan.
- Work with your advisor to create an estate plan *now* to protect your assets for yourself and your family.
- Choose someone you trust to be your executor or the trustee of your trust.
- Name your retirement account beneficiaries—both primary and contingent—on beneficiary forms (not in your will).
- If there are multiple beneficiaries for one asset (an IRA, for example), make sure that each beneficiary's share is clearly identified with a fraction, a percentage, or the word *equally* if that is applicable.

- Name beneficiaries for your other property (both primary and contingent) in your will, including instructions for taking care of minor children or passing specific property that may have no financial value but is important to you.
- Give items that generally don't belong in a will, such as photographs and ornaments, to the people you want to have them while you are living.
- Take advantage of the annual exclusion gifts to give assets to your beneficiaries while you are still living if you anticipate an estate tax problem down the road.

Chapter 14

PUTTING IT ALL TOGETHER

Action is the foundational key to all success.

—Pablo Picasso

So there you have it—how to get rich and how to stay rich *for life.*

Keep in mind that I haven't recommended what stocks to buy or what mutual funds to invest in, whether to buy and hold or sell and get into real estate, cash, or gold. Nor have I suggested specific life insurance products for you to look into. These are decisions to talk over and make with your respective confessors—the expert professional advisors I have shown you how to find, who can guide you and help you successfully implement the solutions required to keep you from sinking when the government S.H.I.P. hits the fan and taxes soar.

Remember what I wrote at the outset of this book: It's a brave new world out there, and you are on your own insofar as securing your financial present *and* your financial future are concerned.

As I've shown, financial well-being has become like a football game. And there's a philosophy in football that says: Your score at halftime is irrelevant; give me your score at the end of the game, and I'll tell you who won.

The same philosophy applies to staying rich for life.

You now know that the first half of the game is all about accumulating wealth to enjoy and to keep building up throughout your lifetime. You likewise understand that the second half is about keeping as much as you can of your unspent wealth from disappearing into the voracious maw of the IRS at the time when you need those assets most—in retirement. But too many people just quit at halftime, walking off the field to shower and celebrate with champagne, thinking they've got the money game licked. Meanwhile, the IRS comes out onto the field to play the third and fourth quarters with no opposition, and it winds up winning the game instead. This happens all the time.

But it's not going to happen to you, is it?

You know what you have to do. You have to play all four quarters. You have to build up your score and then execute your strategy for holding onto your lead so that you wind up winning the game. And now you know how. Once you have a plan in place, you will be able to spend and enjoy your money. You'll be able to make that happen by following my five-step plan, which I have detailed throughout this book. There's only one more piece of advice I can offer: *Just do it!*

Keep more of your money by moving it, one step at a time, from accounts that are forever taxed to accounts that are never taxed. There's no reason you shouldn't end up with *more* than Uncle Sam. You want your money free and clear forever. That happens only by taking action to create and follow *your* plan, not the government's plan, on your terms and timeline, not the government's.

Now start spending and enjoying your money. It's okay. Even "Dear Abby" agrees.

> *"Good resolutions are simply checks that men draw*
> *on a bank where they have no account."*
> —OSCAR WILDE

TOP FAQs . . .

"Dear Abby,

My husband hates to spend money! I cut my own hair and make my own clothes, and I have to account for every nickel I spend. Meanwhile he has a stack of savings bonds put away that would choke a cow. How do I get some money out of him before we are both called to our final judgment? He says he's saving for a rainy day.

Forty Years Hitched"

"Dear Forty Years Hitched,

Tell him it's raining!

Abby"

Abby is right, as usual. *It's raining now.* So it's up to you—you don't want to disappoint yourself or your loved ones, who are counting on you. Jacques Plante, a goalie who played in the National Hockey League years ago, once said: "How would you like to have a job where every time you make a mistake, a red light goes on, a siren sounds, and 15,000 people boo?" Well, if you mess up your financial planning now, you might not get fifteen thousand boos, just one big one from your family—and it will be much louder!

Don't sit on the sidelines like a friend of mine who makes the same New Year's resolution every year. He always resolves to join a gym, which he does, but then he complains, "I wrote the check to join the fitness club. The check cleared and I haven't lost an ounce. What a rip-off!" "But you actually have to go there and exercise!" I tell him.

Writing a check or just reading this book is only the beginning. Now you have to follow up with action. Don't be like the fellow who came to me after his mother passed away and said that his inheritance had been wiped out by taxes and costly mistakes. "How did this happen?" he asked me. "My mother went to your seminar!" I remembered her and answered, "Yes, she did go to my seminar, but all she did was eat!"

The ancient Greeks said that suffering arises from trying to control what is uncontrollable and from neglecting what is within our power to control. They were right. The means to stay rich for life are in your power to control, but only if you take action now. Tomorrow is too late!

That is how you end up with More, More, More—more money for you to enjoy now, more for your retirement, and more for your loved ones.

And more of it *tax free*.

That's how you *stay rich for life*!

Acknowledgments

You can accomplish anything in life,
provided that you do not mind who gets the credit.
—Harry S. Truman

Thanks to my dad. He is no longer with us, but he continues to be a positive influence on me. I am still learning from him.

Thank you to all of my clients over the years. The best parts of this book are the real-life stories, both good and bad, that come from years of working with all of you. Readers will reap the benefits of your experiences so they don't have to learn the hard way.

Bob Marty produced and directed my latest Public Broadcasting Service television special, *Stay Rich for Life!*, the companion program for this book. Bob is not only *one* of the best, but in my humble opinion he is *the* best producer there is. Bob was also the producer and director of my first PBS program, *Stay Rich Forever & Ever with Ed Slott,* which became yet another in the collection of Bob's many hit shows. Attaboy, Bob! Thanks also for helping to get this book going and keeping the process on track.

In addition, Bob Marty spent hours, not only in the editing room for my PBS shows, but on the phone interviewing some of the top financial minds in the country for this book, so that we could include their diverse views and planning strategies to help you to both accumulate wealth and keep it protected. Bob also designed the logos and artwork for the book and the television program. Thanks, Bob, for your hard work on this project. Thanks also to Julie, Bob's wife, for loaning him to us.

Thank you to Christina Morano, Bob Marty's incredibly talented production and editing expert. Thanks for your dedication to our programs. Add this to your list of credits.

John McCarty is a great writer, period. John has been my collaborator on all my recent books, but he really had his work cut out for him with this one. Not only did he go through all of the interview transcripts and make them both informative and readable, but he also conducted some of the interviews himself. In addition to all of that, he did his usual great job of polishing my writing, and he managed all of this under incredible time constraints. Thank you, John, for a superb performance under extreme pressure. Thanks also to John's wife, Cheryl, for answering our phone calls at all hours of the day and night!

Thanks to Terrel Cass, president and general manager of WLIW21 New York Public Television, and to Laura Savini, vice president of marketing and communications. WLIW was the first public television station to broadcast my program. What's more special to me is that WLIW21 happens to be my own public television station, of which I am a proud supporter.

In addition, thank you to all the great people at all the public television stations around the country for airing my program and helping to make it a success. I hope my new special based on this book continues to help all these great PBS stations raise much-needed pledge dollars to continue their mission—one that I share—of informing, educating, and entertaining their audiences.

Laurin Levine is the managing partner of our companies and is also to be credited with making this book and our public television programs a reality. They would not have happened without her persistence and belief in me. She has also spent hours and weekends proofreading every word of this book and making key changes to more clearly explain certain points—especially in Chapter 10,

"Money and Women." Laurin has worked with me for years and never ceases to amaze me with her business-building and relationship skills. I am able to do what I do only because Laurin handles everything else for me, including making wise business decisions, and I am thankful for that. Thank you, Laurin, for believing in me and sharing my vision. Thank you also for keeping our growing company together and, most important, for being my friend for all these years. I look forward to sharing future successes with you.

Thank you to Margot Reilly, our controller and a top-notch accountant. Thanks also to Michael Lichter, CPA, who runs our tax and accounting practice. Margot and Mike have been with me for almost twenty years, helping clients—and me, too. Thanks to both of you for your years of exceptional work.

Thanks to our team of IRA experts, whom I believe are the best in the business:

Beverly DeVeny
Denise Appleby
Marvin Rotenberg

Thank you to all of the hardworking, loyal, and enthusiastic people we work with. We really do have a great team.

Ryan Fortese is our director of operations and runs all of our outside programs and marketing. His team includes these fantastic people:

Patrick Wherry
Kira Tullio
Jared Trexler
Jane Lurie

I want to thank the great people who work in our office and at our advisor training programs and seminars. They also make for a great team: Glenda Zolezzi, Pat Pakus, Liliana Epstein, Rachel Slott, Pamela Daum, Ellen Spergel, and Jeffrey Levine.

Thank you to our outside conference and program coordinators Frank Quiles and Mary Rispoli from Conference Direct. Frank Quiles is our on-site specialist, and nothing is ever too much for him to coordinate. No matter what the situation—and there are many that develop at the various hotels and event sites—Frank's response is always "It's my pleasure." Working with you is *our* pleasure. Thank you, Frank!

Thanks to Debbie Slott, our graphic artist. She makes everything we do look better. I look at some of the brochures she designs, and I want to sign up myself! Thanks, Debbie.

Thank you to Jane von Mehren, my fantastic publisher at Random House Publishing Group Trade Paperbacks. Add this to the list of books that Jane has worked on with me. Jane has a tireless team at Random House, all of whom helped to get this book completed at warp speed and whom I also thank:

Gina Centrello, Publisher, Random House Publishing Group
Libby McGuire, Publisher, Ballantine Books
Kim Hovey, Associate Publisher, Ballantine Books, Random
    House Trade Paperbacks
Christina Duffy, Editor, Ballantine Books
Marketing: Sanyu Dillon and Stacey Witcraft
Publicity: Brian McLendon and Amanda Ice
Sales: Jack Perry, Kelle Ruden, and Allyson Pearl
Production: Shona McCarthy, Sarah Feightner, Benjamin
    Dreyer, Mark Maguire, Lisa Feuer, Grant Neumann,
    Carole Lowenstein, and Mary Wirth
Art: Beck Stvan and Michelle Taormina

Thank you very much for the financial and legal advisors who agreed to be interviewed for this book. One thing I know for sure is that no one can know it all. But the miracle is this: You don't have to know it all if you know enough people who know some of it. I am fortunate to know the advisors listed here. Together, they have hundreds of years of experience, and I thank them for so generously sharing their valuable time and thoughts for this book:

William Nelson

Joseph "Big Joe" Clark

W. Michael Robertson

Deborah Linscott

Debra DeMarie

Beth L. Blecker

Sandeep Varma

Dean Barber

Michael Brown

Seymour Goldberg

David Buckwald

Denise Appleby

I want to acknowledge and thank the members of Ed Slott's Elite IRA Advisor Group, especially during these turbulent times. While many advisors have run for the hills, these advisors have continued their dedication to education and expertise. They believe in serving their clients by looking at the big, long-term picture and doing the best they can to provide value and financial security for their clients. They invest in their education, and that is desperately needed. You should expect no less from your advisor.

I would like to acknowledge the following groups and individuals, who have continually supported my mission to provide consumers and advisors with the highest level of advice and education. Thank you to:

MDRT (Million Dollar Round Table)

TOT (Top of the Table)

NAIFA (National Association of Insurance and Financial Advisors)

AALU (Association for Advanced Life Underwriting)

AICPA (American Institute of Certified Public Accountants)

The New York State Society of CPAs

The National Conference of CPA Practitioners

The Estate Planning Council of New York City, Inc.

Dan Sullivan and Dan Taylor at The Strategic Coach

Financial Planning magazine, including Marion Asnes, Dan Goldemen, Pat Durner, and Stacy Schultz

Stephan R. Leimberg, Leimberg Information Services, Inc., www.leimbergservices.com

Natalie Choate, JD, Nutter McClennen & Fish, LLP www.ataxplan.com

Michael J. Jones, CPA, Thompson Jones, LLP

Bob Keebler, shareholder in the accounting firm Virchow, Krause & Company, LLP

Bruce Steiner, attorney with Kleinberg, Kaplan, Wolff & Cohen, PC

Barry C. Picker, CPA/PFS, CFP®

Sidney Kess

Martin Shenkman, Esq.

Gregory Kolojeski and Jane Schuck, of Brentmark Software

James Lange, Esq.

Joseph L. Cicchinelli, CPA, MBA, PMC www.pmc-corp.com

Mary Kay Foss, CPA, Marzluft, Tulis & Foss CPAs

Shannon Evans, JD, LLM

Kelly McCarty, Brokers International, Ltd.

Michael D. Walters and Brent D. Enders, USA Financial

Gary Reed, David Gaylor, and Rodney Harris—The 3-Mentors

Van Mueller, LUTCF, and host of www.vanmueller.com

Marc A. Silverman, CLU, ChFC

Mehdi Fakharzadeh, Met Life

David Malkin, CLU, ChFC of NJL & C

Mike Reidy, Nationwide Financial

John O'Gara, New York Life

Bob Ellwanger, New York Life

Sanford Fisch, founder and CEO of the American Academy of Estate Planning Attorneys

Thanks to Donald Jay Korn, one of the best tax and financial writers I know. Don has been interviewing and writing for years, not only for my IRA newsletter *Ed Slott's IRA Advisor,* but you will also see his work in countless financial publications. Thanks for all your help, Don.

Thank you to my wife, Linda, and my children, Ilana (Go Gators!) and Rachel (Go FTSK!). When you see this book, you'll know what I was doing in my office all that time. Thank you for allowing me to pursue my work, especially when it so often takes me away from all of you. I can't wait to get home and go to Pizzaiola with you.

Thanks, Mom. You're my biggest fan. Thanks for a lifetime of cheering, "That's my son!"

tax exemption for, 160, 165–67,
174–75, 179, 189
types of, 169–71
life span
financial resources and, 114–15,
118, 120, 165
for women vs. men, 125
living trusts
attorneys handling, 63
function of, 191
funding, xii
living wills, 194
lotteries, 78, 83
lump-sum withdrawals
from 401(k), 48, 149, 150
at retirement, 24, 149
rollovers of, 130
tax break for, 149, 162

M

married couples
capital losses and, 147
estate settlements and,
181–82
estate tax exemption and, 161,
194
financial decisions for,
124–25
home sales and, 148
life insurance and, 178
as mutual beneficiaries, 190
Roth IRA contributions by,
104
same-sex, 187

matching funds for company
401(k) plans, 12, 80, 104
Medicare
eligibility for, 11
funding for, 8
Microsoft Money software, 77
mistakes
in estate planning, 192–95
in investment portfolios, 90–92
as learning opportunities,
xviii–xx
in retirement account
withdrawals, 152–56
in tax payment, xvi
with women's finances,
131–33
Moneydance software, 77
Morningstar, 21
mutual funds
as income investments, 87
as investing start, 34

N

National Association of Enrolled
Agents (NAEA), 52
National Conference of CPA
Practitioners, 51
national debt, 100
National Endowment for Financial
Education, 21
net unrealized appreciation
(NUA)
company stock and, 149
CPA expertise with, 48

ABOUT THE AUTHOR

ED SLOTT is a nationally recognized retirement account tax expert and a professional speaker at conferences nationwide. He hosts www.irahelp.com, which provides retirement resources for both consumers and professional advisors. He created Ed Slott's Elite IRA Advisor Group,™ an exclusive registry of financial advisors. Slott is the author of *Your Complete Retirement Planning Road Map*, *Parlay Your IRA into a Family Fortune*, and *The Retirement Savings Time Bomb and How to Defuse It*. He publishes *Ed Slott's IRA Advisor*, a monthly newsletter for financial professionals. He is a frequent contributor to such publications as *The New York Times*, *The Washington Post*, *The Wall Street Journal*, *Newsweek*, *Fortune*, *Forbes*, *Money*, and *USA Today*, and has been a frequent guest on national television. He lives on Long Island.